HEALING EVE

*The Woman's Journey
from Religious Fundamentalism
to Spiritual Freedom*

DR. JIMMY LAURA SMULL

Aug: 1, 2005

*To David Feinstein —
Thank you for your
support and encouragement
to carry on the
work of personal
mythology.
Sincerely,
Jimmy Laura Smull*

AMP&RSAND, INC.
Chicago, Illinois

First Edition

ISBN 0-9761235-1-7

Book Design: David Robson, Robson Design
Cover Art: Guy Billout
Cover Design: Tom Moyer, M1 partnership
Author Photo: Figge Photography

Published by Ampersand, Inc., Chicago, Illinois

Printed in the United States of America

CALL TO ACTION

The research laid bare in this book gives us the information we need as a society to understand the inner workings of all fanatical organizations. Churches and religious institutions to which we were entrusted as young girls bear the primary responsibility for our unnecessary pain, and it is to them that my appeal is directed.

To our religious leaders: note that all of the women in my study have left the church. They are brilliant, passionate, loving, caring women. This did not have to happen. We are your daughters, your wives, your mothers. In the name of God's love, we deserve to be healed, not punished. I call upon you to search your own souls and rectify the damage that has been and continues to be done to women every day in the name of God. We can and must work together to heal Eve.

DR. JIMMY LAURA SMULL
LAGUNA BEACH, CALIFORNIA

DEDICATION

To my granddaughter, Niki.
May you always have
the freedom to choose.

CONTENTS

ACKNOWLEDGMENTS

Three components made this book possible—the participants, my colleagues, and my family and friends.

Without the participants there would be no book. I am merely a facilitator of their desire to share their stories. They were willing to revisit the pain of their experience with religious fundamentalism, hoping that someone else might have the courage to leave their oppressive religious systems. For your bravery, I am deeply indebted to all of you.

Once I was able to articulate where I thought I was headed toward my doctorate, Cultural Anthropologist, Dr. Marlene DeRios, pointed me toward Saybrook Research and Graduate School. One of the reasons I chose Saybrook was because of Dr. Stanley Krippner, world-renowned for his work in consciousness studies and his breakthrough model, who had collaborated with Dr. David Feinstein, an expert in personal mythology. Other professors at Saybrook contributed to the steps I took toward attaining my goal. I am indebted to President, Dr. Maureen O'Hara; Don Cooper; Dr. Donald Rothberg; Dr. Marcia Salner; my committee, Dr. Arne Collen and Dr. Ilene Serlin, who helped me fine-tune my dissertation; and of course, to Dr. Stanley Krippner, my chair, mentor, and cheerleader. I was also encouraged by Dr. Stephen Larsen, New York, to convert my dissertation into a book. My other colleagues who had been through the process and led the way for me are Dr. Jo Anne Van Tilburg, Dr. Tessa Warschaw, Dr. Cherilyn Sheets and Wilma Friesema, MFCC.

Certainly, I am so grateful for my husband, Les Smull, who removed all barriers between me and my dream. His vision of the importance of my work prevented me from the thought of ever giving up. My children, also, encouraged me at every turn—son, Jack and daughter-in-law, Carolyn; step-daughter, Lauren and son-in-law, Bob; step-daughter, Kerri and son-in-law, Tom; and six beautiful grandchildren—Nicolette, Matthew, Lowell, Oliver, Robert, and Alexander, who wondered if their grandmother would ever get out of school!

My friends believed in me more than I did in myself at times. My best friend, Theo Cox, encouraged my dream, loved me, and served as my analyst throughout the whole process. I thank my right-hand assistant, Jane Sweeney. My other cheerleaders included Barbara Taylor, Jennifer James, Ph.D, June Weir, Dana Davis, Lydia Rosenberger, Pamela Primm, Rita Vogt, and Chloe Eaton.

I had a team of spiritual leaders who loved and encouraged me, including Carol Lovejoy, Jheri St. James, Carol Dryer, and Reverend Karen Boland—thank you for your enlightenment.

This book is in memory of Susan Atkinson Tietz, who left this world way too soon, but left behind for her friends an enthusiasm for women to realize their dreams. She read my manuscripts, sent me the most encouraging cards and letters, and made me feel like such a heroine in an effort to free women from the ties that bound them.

Finally, to my parents, who, although they were behind the veil of fundamentalism until their deaths, expressed their love for me in every way possible. I am honored to call you Mother and Daddy.

In closing, my deepest love and admiration go to my Muse—you know who you are and how much I am indebted to you.

DR. JIMMY LAURA SMULL
LAGUNA BEACH, CALIFORNIA

Two Women, One Heart

The tree is in full bloom for all to gaze
Knows that it all comes together in mysterious ways.
JIMMY LAURA SMULL

I had been invited to interview Teresa in her tiny adobe dwelling
as part of my doctoral research. We had been talking all day,
the shadows falling around us, but we made no attempt to turn
on any lights. This beautiful elder, granddaughter of the
reservation's Mother Corn, had finally stopped sobbing out the 51
years of pent-up resentment that had taken root so long ago. It was,
not coincidentally, 51 years ago when two spinster missionaries had
arrived at her adobe's door, offering her needy mother food, used
clothing and a new God.

The subject of my dissertation was women who had broken free
from fundamentalist religion to find spiritual freedom. Primarily, I
interviewed women whose associations were with fundamentalist
and/or evangelical Baptist, Methodist, Pentecostal and Lutheran
denominations. Teresa and I were both raised Baptists, an orthodox
form of Protestant Christianity. However, while completing my
dissertation, I also encountered a number of women who had
escaped Catholic and non-Christian fundamentalism, as well. These
included extremist Islamic and Jewish orthodoxies as well as a
variety of psychological and spiritual sects.

Despite the fact that I had been personally invited by Teresa —
and that she was aware of the fact that we both had advanced
degrees — when I first appeared on her front stoop, she recoiled.
With my coiffed blond hair and tailored outfit, I unwittingly revived
in her the memories of those two corseted missionaries of long ago.
The two bearers of word of God's salvation had been sent to the
reservation by a Baptist church, not dissimilar to the one in which I
had been raised. Until the bearers of this toxic version of Christian

love visited her mother's adobe, Teresa's family had followed the traditional ways.

"We were taught that we lived in a world where all things were alive: the trees, rocks, mountains, clouds, all of these things were vital, and we took these things in through what we called the Breath." At eight years of age, Teresa was sat down by the missionaries and told that such thoughts were blasphemy: an affront to God. The missionaries took her family in hand, purified them of their Native American beliefs and customs and replaced them with the values, rules and practices of Christian fundamentalism. Prominent among the new teachings: the belief that because of Eve's sin in the Garden of Eden, Teresa and the women in her life were doomed. Their lives would be dominated by abusive men and patriarchal systems. "Because Eve ate the forbidden fruit and tempted Adam to do the same, all women would be punished with the pain of childbirth and a life of toil and misery," she had been told. Unhappily, this sentiment is put forth by fundamentalist versions of all Abrahamic religions that are rooted in their own toxic interpretations of this common mythology.

Teresa could not control her tears as she remembered the day her mother returned home from her first shopping trip with her new missionary friends. The traditional hand-beaded dress her mother had been wearing was in a bag. Instead, her mother was uncomfortably sporting a brand new corset, pillbox hat and little white gloves. From that day forward, Teresa spent much of her lifetime struggling with the destructive force of an absolute truth that relentlessly denied her own.

Now an elder, she had left fundamentalism behind, working hard to reclaim a sense of her own authenticity. It was Teresa who had volunteered to become one of my research subjects a year previously—at the beginning of my doctoral work. At the time, I was with a group of students touring the archeology and cultural mythology of pueblos in the southwest, and Teresa had been our guide. After several weeks of going from village to village, my blue jeans had turned the color of dust, my fingernails caked with mud. This was the picture of me Teresa had in mind when she eagerly anticipated my visit. While intellectually Teresa had been prepared—even enthusiastic—about the opportunity to share her journey from fundamentalism to freedom with a fellow academic, she hadn't expected to confront ghosts from her past standing at her door in my designer shoes and matching bag.

"You look like one of them," Teresa greeted me apprehensively, taking in my starched outfit and smooth hands, hands that had obviously never fed the pigs, swept the clay floor, put wood into the pot stove. *"How can I possibly see you as anybody other than the enemy?"*

"I guess we'll just have to let our hearts talk." I responded.

The particular movement within which both Teresa and I were raised was first officially referred to as "Christian fundamentalism" in the 1920s when a group of dissenters aimed to defend what they defined as true Christianity against liberal Christians influenced by modern thoughts and standards. By the 1940s and '50s, the era of my childhood, Christian fundamentalism had become an established way of being. It dominated large parts of Texas and the South. Enthusiastic believers, inspired by "The Great Commission" to spread the word of Salvation to non-believers, reached out to heathens wherever they could be found. And so it was that the two corseted missionaries came out of my world to forge their way deep into "Indian country" and into Teresa's family adobe.

Warily at first, Teresa and I began sharing memories. It didn't take long to realize that we were exactly the same age. In fact, we were both exactly ten years old when we had been taught a hymn we sang every Sunday called "Blest Be the Tie That Binds."

Blest be the tie that binds
Our hearts in Christian love
The fellowship of kindred minds
Is like to that above.

As the conversation deepened, I felt that she was no longer seeing me as the enemy. True, I had sung the song in a church that resembled the great cathedrals in Europe, 100-member choir and massive multi-piped organ, while Teresa sang hers to the wheezy notes pumped by the two missionaries out of a portable organ. But as "recovering fundamentalists," we shared so much in common! Before long, Teresa's eight-year-old nephew dropped by. He came, bearing two Christmas presents for his Aunt, all smiles when she gave him some gifts in return. Then she asked him to sing with her a traditional Indian song she had recently taught him. Past, present and future were woven into a tapestry of love that gave me a glimpse of the richness and vitality of her reclaimed life.

Until my meeting with Teresa, I hadn't fully realized how pervasive were the issues that I thought had been my own private hell. Nor did I realize how diverse were the populations affected: how similar the woundings. At the very moment I had seen the look of horror pass over Teresa's face as I stood in the doorway of her adobe, I had become far more than a curious scholar studying disaffected fundamentalists for a research project. I realized that, in fact, I had become a woman willing to take on hell itself, to rectify the wrongs of the past and to help others reclaim lives of freedom, integrity and authenticity beyond the toxic world of fundamentalism in whatever form.

On the surface, my own fundamentalist community looked very different from the one within which Teresa found herself embedded. In my case, I was raised by my well-educated father—vice-president of a leading oil company—and my mother, a housewife who socialized regularly at the local women's clubs. We attended a liberal Methodist church until I was the age of nine. My parents were persuaded by old friends to visit one of the country's largest Baptist churches, which happened to be in our hometown. The experience overwhelmed them emotionally. They found themselves swept up in the moment, walking down the aisle to the podium where they repented their sins. My life soon centered around the church, attending services, classes, church choir and camp as well as proselytizing friends and neighbors. There was no more dancing or playing cards as my family devoted ourselves to "working out our sinfulness." My mother held me by the hand as she warned Jewish neighbors that they were going to hell, adding that the entire continent of Africa, as well as the parents of one of my friends who owned a liquor store, were likewise doomed. So were the Indian children whose clothes I supplied. Unless they come to accept Jesus along with my hand-me-down frocks, which was the point of our charity, they were doomed, too.

As a teen-ager, I attended the fundamentalist Baylor University, answering prohibitions against pre-marital sex with an ill-conceived early marriage. Ironically, this marriage was the beginning of my digging out from beneath the burden of fundamentalism. I gave birth to my son and followed my husband's career to California. There, exposed to outside influences, at the age of 27 I mustered the courage to divorce my husband and leave the church. Out of sight from the watchful eyes of my home church community, I began to explore a new world of options and opportunities, basking in the company of healthier attitudes and enjoying the freedom that had been denied me for too long.

For years, I had kept my painful childhood experiences in the fundamentalist environment, and my break from the church through the difficult and forbidden divorce, a secret. Eventually, I finally met and married a successful businessman outside the church who had a mature attitude about religion. We raised our son free of fundamentalism and engrained feelings of unworthiness. I sought out a secular education for myself that led to a license in real estate.

Grappling seriously with my spiritual recovery, I organized a conference for 200 women in New York on the subject of "Body, Mind and Spirit of Women." When the subject matter turned to "spirit," I was amazed at how many women took advantage of the opportunity to vent disillusionment with fundamentalism. They represented a wide range of religious formulations.

It was as a doctoral student at Saybrook Research and Graduate School that I encountered the literature that gave me a conceptual framework for expressing that which I had only previously experienced as intuition and feelings. Foremost among my influences was the work of the man who was to become my dissertation advisor, psychologist and former president of the Association for Humanistic Psychology, Dr. Stanley Krippner. While I could find no book specifically dedicated to the subject of women breaking free from fundamentalism, I found myself intellectually and emotionally at home in the world of psychological/sociological and anthropological analysis to which I had been introduced. I was particularly interested in the field of cultural mythology. In academic terms, it describes a model by which human beings experience their lives as having meaning. This was very different from our everyday notions of myth as a fictional story from ancient times.

Dr. Krippner, in the book he co-authored with Dr. David Feinstein, *Personal Mythology: The Psychology of Your Evolving Self*, as well as in his lectures and papers, identified a process, and in particular a personal mythology, occurring naturally in the course of healthy development, by which human beings recognize and discard belief systems that no longer serve them. That's stage one. The sense of breaking free typically comes as the result of a crisis, resulting in a period of disillusionment—stage two. Ultimately, the healthy individual brings his or her original and disillusioned worldview into what the scholars call "synthesis." In this third stage, the individual is freed to retrieve valuable elements from all periods of her life, assembling a mature worldview marked by authenticity and meaning.

Inspired, at every opportunity, I began working with the material, applying it to my own circumstances. Eventually, I began to formulate my own model and process along with my associate, Dr. Carol Orsborn—with whom I have subsequently co-authored a book titled *The Silver Pearl*. This is the model I tested against the women in my research study, seeing in them consistent evidence of our collective abilities to a) recognize toxic patterns carried forward from our childhoods and b) marshall energies away from self-condemnation, toward positive change.

I devoted several years of study as well as the bulk of a year driving and flying around the country to meet women who had escaped primarily from Protestant fundamentalism, as well as others who had broken away from various fundamentalist formulations to find spiritual freedom. *Had other women found a way to dig through layers of toxic beliefs to reclaim their souls? Were their experiences similar to mine? Had they come out whole or scarred?* In homes, speaking in quick sentences sandwiched between the cries of babies, in dimly-lit adobes and posh hotel suites, what I discovered amazed, shocked and saddened me. At their core, our stories are all so similar. Many pieces fit neatly and make perfect sense to all of us; other times all we can do is shake our heads and wonder how we ever survived. Often there is the hope of on-going spiritual progress as our journeys continue to unfold; other times our memories seem to threaten to engulf us in shadows left over from the emotions we have struggled so hard to leave behind. However, we had arrived at this moment. Each of us had been raised as fundamentalists, and each had ultimately found herself on the path to freedom. When I returned, I presented my findings to Dr. Krippner who was amazed at the breadth and depth of what I had discovered.

While my dedication to this subject matter grew with each interview, each page of my dissertation and now this book, it was in Teresa's adobe that I realized that I had embarked not only on my Ph.D., but my life's work. This book represents the next step in my journey, using Teresa's and my life stories, as well as those of dozens of women I interviewed in-depth and scores more I surveyed, to help others like us find their way to reclaiming their souls.

This book has a happy ending, by the way. Even though we were all threatened by fundamentalism, each of us found our way back to authentic identities and lives of meaning after we left. Having turned our backs on religious dogma, what we now embrace is not within walls: it is our personal style of expressing our spiritual selves. When I think back to my interview with Teresa, I recall with warmth and hope Teresa's easy ability to exchange Christmas gifts with her nephew while singing with him a song from her own Native American tradition. In my own life, I have been blessed with the ability to derive comfort from some elements of the childhood traditions I had left behind. But I no longer fear that I am damned to hell if I think for myself. Most of all, I am blessed by my belief in the inherent goodness of humanity and faith in a God who loves me unconditionally.

In the midst of my doctoral coursework, I blocked out time alone for a writing retreat. My goal was to write an essay titled "The Experience of Disillusionment with One's Personal Mythology." Before I could even open my first resource book, I found myself instead rushing to put pen to paper. As for the first time in my life, a poem poured out of me. I recognized in this poem a message from the depths of my heart, representing an integration of all of the pieces of my authentic life experience.

Life is a fabric which is woven from beginning to end
A tree's life is similar—and branches should blend

Life must honor its roots from which it grows
Just as the tree takes its lumps—only the strong ones will last

Life has a story to tell if anyone will listen
Just as the tree reveals its story on branches that glisten

The fabric of life woven so tight
Looks back and says it doesn't matter who's wrong or who's right

The tree is in full bloom for all to gaze
Knows that it all comes together in mysterious ways.

It is with this poem in my heart that I honor your quest to find increased resolution and freedom in your life.

DR. JIMMY LAURA SMULL
LAGUNA BEACH, CALIFORNIA, 2005

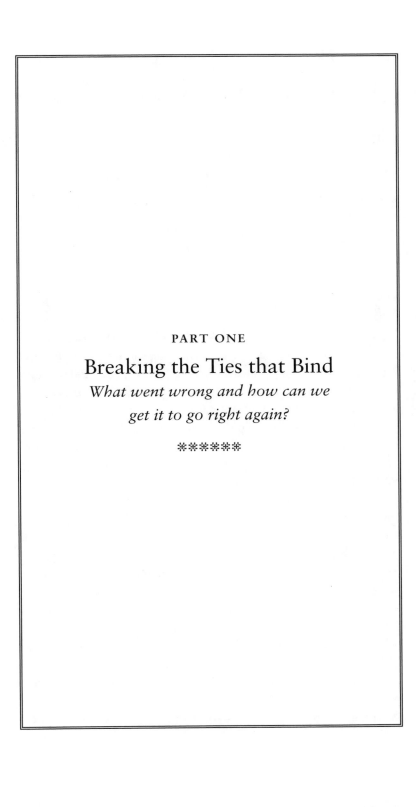

PART ONE

Breaking the Ties that Bind
*What went wrong and how can we
get it to go right again?*

✻✻✻✻✻✻

CHAPTER ONE

Jimmy Laura Smull: A Soul Submerged

And unto Adam he said Because thou has hearkened unto
the voice of thy wife, and hast eaten of the tree,
of which I commanded thee, saying, Thou shalt not eat of it:
cursed is the ground for thy sake; In sorrow shalt thou
eat of it all the days of thy life.
GENESIS (3:17–19)

The ten-year-old girl walks alone through a huge church toward the one light illuminating the baptismal pool. She is robed in white and painfully aware of the thousands of eyes upon her. Descending the baptismal steps into chest-high water, her mind is swimming. Somewhere in the crowd, her Sunday school teacher, her parents and their family's new friends are beaming at the child's first admission of sinfulness.

For weeks, after spending the bulk of her childhood believing that she was good enough and loved just as she was, she has been pressured to repent and be cleansed through baptism. Angry and ashamed, she is unable to understand why it is that God is suddenly so mad at her and why she has to do something this scary to appease him. The frightened little girl scans the church, not for friendly faces — but for a way out. Finding none, she enters the chilling water, telling herself that enduring this is the price of belonging. Before she can catch a breath, the preacher invokes a prayer. Pinching the child's nose, he plunges her beneath the water. In that split second, the child finds herself agonizing over which fear is worse: the threat of being accidentally drowned by the preacher or the promise that she will be doomed to an eternity in hell if she somehow struggles to break free and makes a run for it.

I, Jimmy Laura Smull, know the secret-most thoughts of the ten-year-old on her way to becoming a full-fledged member of one of the largest, most prestigious Baptist churches in Texas because I was that little girl. And even now, despite the over fifty years that have passed, the earning of my doctorate and the birthing and raising of a child of my own to adulthood, I still weep for the loss of my innocence in the name of the God who was meant to save me. When I chose women disaffected from religious fundamentalism as the subject matter of my doctoral dissertation, I was more than a curious scholar. As a second-career graduate student, I selected the topic because I, too, had become a woman who'd been willing to take on hell itself to recover a life of freedom, integrity and authenticity beyond the grasp of the particular formulation of doctrine and tradition known as Christian fundamentalism.

I wasn't born into fundamentalism. Rather, I was raised by my well-educated father—vice president of a leading oil company—and my mother, a social housewife who took great joy in meeting up with friends at our city's blue chip women's clubs. We attended a liberal Methodist church until I reached the age of nine. I remember that church as a fun and inviting place to go, where my parents would meet up with many of the same friends with whom they socialized and worked. My parents even drank socially from time to time and played a little cards. Both my younger brother and I loved to watch my parents and their friends whirling around the floor at the occasional square-dance. We were happy.

THE GATES OF HELL

I admit that as a nine-year-old, I wasn't privy to whatever dark clouds may have been lurking beneath what I thought of as the happy part of my childhood. But foreshadowed or not, I remember the first time our family went as guests of some old friends to visit one of the largest Baptist churches in Texas. It was the end of happiness and my introduction to life camped out at the gates of hell. I can remember every detail of the first Sunday morning service we attended, the minister, a world-renowned conservative Christian fundamentalist, presiding. Escorted by my parents' old friends, our family entered into the huge sanctuary, above us a wrap-around balcony and before us, the largest choir I had ever seen. Everything was bigger than life, the skillfully orchestrated interplay of prayer, sermons and music manipulating the emotions into an all-consuming climax calling for those attending the service to be convicted of their sins. My brother and I were wide-eyed as we watched a seemingly never-ending stream of weeping, moaning and shouting people moving through the pews and up the center aisle, throwing themselves on their knees and begging to be saved. Then suddenly, we watched in shocked horror as our very own parents brushed past us to join the parade of sinners. In the distance, we could see them on their knees repenting their sins, making their profession of faith and joining the church. Here was the vice president of a leading oil company and my sociable mother handing over control of their family's lives to the church. Astonished as I was at the time, I had no idea of what a complete transformation this would come to represent.

From that moment on, my life centered on the church, attending services on Sunday morning as well as Wednesday and Sunday nights. There were Sunday school classes, Training Union—at which both my parents soon became teachers—church choir practices and performances, church camp and more. Every time the church doors were open, we were there.

Even the potentially mitigating influence of public school offered surprisingly little relief. When I was in grammar school, a committee of Christian fundamentalists was given permission to read every textbook and delete the subject matter that did not correspond to Christian fundamentalist teachings. In particular, the origin of the universe, even in science class, was attributed to creationism. I did not read, hear about or have reason to suspect the existence of an alternate theory of evolution, not in grammar school, middle and high school, and even years later when I attended a Christian fundamentalist university.

DISAPPEARING INTO THE CHURCH

Our whole family disappeared into that church, my father soon being named a deacon while my mother took up missionary work in our neighborhood and community. There was no more dancing or playing cards. Even the occasional glass of wine went by the wayside as our family devoted ourselves to "working out our sinfulness." However much we repented, there was always more to do in our never-ending quest for forgiveness. It wasn't until many years later, while interviewing woman after woman for my doctoral research, that I realized that the conviction of my own inferiority—and the on-going quest for perfection—were not just personal shortcomings. Rather, the feelings of mortal inadequacy—the pervasive sense of inferiority that drove us in the failed effort to excel at being a good enough human being—was common to most of the women I interviewed. Their shame and perfectionism had taken root in a variety of religious, spiritual and psychological communities.

Through my research, I set myself to identifying the cause of the painful sense of self shared by all of the women immersed in fundamentalist cultures whom I have known and studied. In brief, I identified the nature and interplay of beliefs to which women in fundamentalism are subjected on an on-going basis. The controlling beliefs can be divided into three major strands woven tightly together: 1) absolute truth; 2) contradictions, mixed messages and hypocrisy; and 3) rigid rules of conduct. In addition, each of these strands carries with it scores of related emotions and feelings— most of them negative. The lives of the women I studied have carried an unfair burden of shame, anger and above all, fear. In future chapters, you will get to know many of these women in detail. But before we continue, here is a brief summary of the three major strands of toxic beliefs.

TOXIC BELIEFS

Absolute Truth All fundamentalists believe that they have exclusive access to absolute truth about the nature of the universe, the meaning of life and the definition of what is right and what is wrong. Christian fundamentalists, in particular, believe that every word of the Bible is inspired by God. The fundamentalist culture holds that their interpretation of this truth cannot be questioned. This is particularly problematical for women since so many of the interpretations are used to assign an inferior, sinful position to women and an elevated power position to men. Absolute truth plays out in problems with exclusivity, black-and-white thinking, perfectionism and judgmental attitudes towards others.

Contradictions, Mixed Messages and Hypocrisy Children in many formulations of fundamentalism are taught that God is loving. Yet in many holy scriptures, they are presented over and over again with the threat of a punishing, vindictive, angry and vengeful God. In Christian fundamentalism, for instance, they are taught that self-love is the sin of pride and cause for damnation. They are told to love their neighbors, but accept that these others will burn in hell forever if they do not convert. They are admonished to love their parents, but are expected to turn against their family if necessary to serve the church. In all fundamentalisms, hypocrisy and mixed messages abound. The individual who raises her voice to question or protest quickly finds herself labeled disloyal.

Rigid Rules of Conduct The belief in absolute truth, compounded by personal feelings of inadequacy related to emotionally unprocessed contradictions, results in a rigid code of behavior. The rules are enforced by the threat of an eternal afterlife in hell. In Christian fundamentalism, due to skewed interpretation of the Bible, the rules cover such wide-ranging issues as church attendance, proselytizing, premarital sex, marriage and children, divorce and remarriage, education and careers.

As I mentioned earlier, in later chapters, you will meet a number of the women I studied. Their life stories illustrate the particular wounds women bound to fundamentalism share, regardless of the particular religion or variation within which they were raised. Using Christian fundamentalism as a case study, it is helpful to note that all formulations in this particular family of fundamentalisms share a common root: the unquestioned premise that the Bible is in its totality inspired by God and must be followed faithfully to the letter or risk going straight to hell. Scripture is cited to support the inspired and absolute nature of the Bible.

All scripture is given by inspiration of God.
II TIMOTHY (3:16–17)

The citation of this and similar passages from the holy books from all religions that claim to be inspired by God is a vital attempt to maintain control over the thinking of the church membership. In accordance with this and similar passages, the scriptures are read, repeated, and memorized to the point that they play over and over again in one's head. Therefore, in any situation in life that one encounters there is immediate recall of a scripture verse dictating the solution. This obedience to absolute truth is particularly problematical for women, as scripture can often be found and cited to assign an inferior, sinful position to women and an elevated power position to men.

SCRIPTURE AND THE WOMAN'S LOT

Several years ago, shortly after embarking on my research project, I was invited to address a group of women at a Baptist church in the Midwest. Having so recently discovered how many others shared my sense of inferiority as a woman formed within fundamentalism, I carefully crafted my speech. I would use fire to fight fire, using scripture centering on women in the Bible to bolster the self-esteem of the women in the audience. I approached the church eagerly, sure that my enthusiasm—supported by my special selection of scripture—would save these women from the pain I had suffered. When I arrived, the audience was abuzz. I took my hostess aside and asked her what was going on. As it turns out, just the day before, scandalized members of the church body had called for a vote. It seems that the minister's wife had been teaching a Sunday school class and that some men in the congregation had chosen to attend along with their wives. The vote came down, pronouncing that it was against Biblical principles for the minister's wife to teach a Sunday school class that had men in attendance.

> *But I suffer not a woman to teach, nor to usurp authority*
> *over the man, but to be in silence.*
> I TIMOTHY (2:12)

A man had been selected to replace her as the new Sunday school teacher.

A couple of years later, while defending my dissertation, one of my committee members challenged me. *Surely, this level of discrimination could not be happening in our day and age?* I assured him that it was still going on, and in fact, presented him with a report in *The New York Times* declaring that as of 1998, the Southern Baptist Convention was holding to the fundamentals that dictated that women remain in a "graciously subservient" position to their husbands.

The article reported on "a declaration on family life" made by the conservative Southern Baptist Convention at their annual meeting in Salt Lake City, Utah. A plea had been made by moderate Baptists to consider a more mainstream evangelical position in which the man and woman are considered equal within the family, with the "headship" no longer being the man. This suggestion was voted down, and the convention amended its statement of beliefs to include "a declaration that a woman should 'submit herself graciously' to her husband's leadership."

A SINISTER INTERPRETATION OF EVE'S SIN

While this was news to my committee, the relegation of women to subservient roles was not new to me. In fact, among my earliest memories within the fundamentalist church was a sinister interpretation of the story of Adam and Eve in Genesis, the first book of the Bible. At the liberal Methodist church of my early childhood, I was familiar with the story. I remembered, in particular, the naming of the animals by Adam and Eve and of course, I knew about Eve eating the forbidden fruit and the couple being forced to leave the Garden of Eden. But in my new Sunday school, I encountered the passage from the Bible for the first time in which God issues his punishment:

Unto the woman he said, I will greatly multiply thy sorrow
and thy conception; in sorrow thou shalt bring forth children;
and thy desire shall be to thy husband,
and he shall rule over thee.
GENESIS (3:16)

This single sentence is packed with fearful implications. Of course, there is what I perceived to be a curse newly placed on my future:

the pain and suffering of childbirth that I would have to bear because of what Eve did so long ago. Motherhood was an exalted concept in the church, and it never occurred to me that I would or could avoid its inevitability. But what should have been a vision of joy and anticipation was perverted into the promise of punishment to come. The idea that pain in childbirth is a natural process for human beings, that drugs could be used to lessen the suffering and that most of the time the mother does not remember the details of the ordeal the moment she holds her precious newborn in her arms, was never entertained. Somehow, the most basic function that we were taught defined the very meaning of our lives as women was inextricably attached to the inspired Biblical story recalling the origins and permanence of the sinfulness and inferiority of the woman. I was ten years old.

And here we arrive at the larger meaning and implications of this oft-quoted passage. Is it any wonder that people in fundamentalist communities who share dark-hued interpretations of the Adam and Eve story view the role of women as being subservient to men in marriage, and also in every other area of church and communal life? Within Christian fundamentalist churches, women are not encouraged or even permitted to be ministers, pastors, or deacons. In the most "obedient" churches, women cannot serve on any governing board in the church, nor serve in any capacity of authority in the church that involves a woman directing men. What can women do, besides bearing children in pain and suffering? Women are expected to serve food and clean up at church activities, teach each other Bible study, and to support the men in the church.

This is the way I was raised as a child in Christian fundamentalism. The male authority figures were ever present, and our minister was elevated to a God-like position. I saw many examples among our church friends that the husbands took their mandate as the head of the woman as an excuse to be abusive and wield their God-given power as they willed. The idea of a "partnership" model for a husband and wife could not be entertained. If there were any doubt on this matter, St. Paul argued the case in his first letter to the Corinthians.

For the man is not of the woman; but the woman of the man.
Neither was the man created for the woman;
but the woman for the man.

I CORINTHIANS (11:8-9)

If giving men supremacy were not enough, the men were also given ample cause to feel resentment and superiority over women, who were seen as the corruptor of otherwise innocent men. These were understandings I had even as a young girl. They were to affect me greatly later in life.

While my father performed as the head of our household, he, himself, was not abusive. In fact, I adored my father. I loved him before we joined the church, and while I was confused by his role in our family's new life, I never doubted that he was a loving man with a generous spirit. But he had become convinced that it was for the ultimate welfare of his family that we follow the dictates of the church to the letter. Years later, after my father's death, my uncle told me that he had confided in him that once he had gone down on his knees to confess his sins, he was frightened by the possibility that any deviation or relapse on his part would have sent him and his family straight to hell: "I don't know if all of what the church teaches us is true, but I'm almost afraid not to believe it if that's the way to heaven," he had said. Unfortunately, baking cookies for fundraisers and clearing the tables at church events was not the end of the roles that the church had in mind for its women.

MISSIONARIES FOR THE CHURCH
Our entire family was charged with the mission to reach out to non-members of our church and encourage them to join us. The Bible verse used to describe this requirement is called "The Great Commission."

Go ye therefore, and teach all nations, baptizing them
in the name of the Father, and of the Son,
and of the Holy Ghost: Teaching them to observe
all things whatsoever I have commanded you...

MATTHEW (28:18-20)

This is understood to mean that every human being must be given the opportunity to accept Christian fundamentalist beliefs. The vastness of such an undertaking requires that everyone, including women, participate in witnessing to others. Although the role of women is restricted within the church, women are encouraged to be assertive and even aggressive outside of the church in the effort to fulfill the Great Commission.

Following this rule was difficult for me. I was very shy, but nevertheless, a fair portion of my time in Sunday school and church camp was invested in teaching me the techniques required to "hook" a potential believer. I dreaded Monday nights, Visitation, when my parents would be given the cards of hapless visitors to the church, many of whom had merely followed their curiosity to a service. Few suspected that the card they were asked to fill out would result in our — or any family—knocking on their door unbidden, begging them to go down on their knees and join us in praying for their salvation. If to my relief no one was at home, we could simply leave our "propaganda" called "The Plan of Salvation" for them, which outlined how one could become a Christian. Otherwise, we were obligated to hand it to them and go over it with them together. The initial pitch was how simple it is to be saved, the "plan" centering around only one Bible verse:

For God so loved the world, that he gave his only begotten Son, that whosoever believeth in him should not perish, but have ever-lasting life.

JOHN (3:16)

The verse quoted above is the very first Bible scripture that a young child is taught, and it is always used in proselytizing or winning lost souls to Jesus. If the "unsaved" did answer the door, I tried to stand in the background and not make my presence known. This ability to fade into the background was one of the few advantages of education within the fundamentalist system that encouraged children to deny and suppress their own impulses, feelings and independent thoughts in order to conform to the pedagogy and agendas imposed by adults. This process has been summarized by one psychologist as "poisonous pedagogy," resulting in the silent, well-behaved child. In later chapters, we will have the opportunity to explore more deeply the psychology of fundamentalist pedagogy, especially as it relates to the education of young girls.

THE QUEST FOR PERFECTION

Proselytizing was unfortunately not confined to Monday nights. In fact, my mother saw it as a particular call to women in the church to make their mark by reaching out to our neighbors, friends and even strangers at just about every possible opportunity.

Not only was this our special job, but a matter of life and death. Or more accurately, of heaven and hell. Since one "mistake" can result in eternal fiery hell for individuals, the Christian fundamentalist feels justified, and indeed feels obligated, to express her judgments to others. Always, the church was on the lookout for mistaken thinking—both on our part, and on those we encountered outside the church. Judgmental attitudes toward others were encouraged, for if the adherent's view is "right," then other views can be confidently judged as "wrong." Much energy is expended by Christian fundamentalists in judging other Christian fundamentalists, as well as non-fundamentalist Christians and non-Christians. In fact, it is as much a sin to withhold the gift of salvation from others as it is to stand apart from the community of believers, itself.

Soon after my baptism, the airport in town wanted to expand, buying out all of the businesses that were adjacent to their land. My father's oil company headquarters was one of these acquisitions. Consequently, the company built a new facility in the northern part of the city. Soon after, we moved into a new house, closer to the offices, in an exclusive area. The house was beautiful and large, even for this neighborhood of big homes, with a grandly manicured back yard. My father planted a gardenia bush right below my bedroom window. In those days, before air conditioning, I cherished the move for providing me with the aroma of gardenias all summer long. Mother cherished something quite different: the opening of this fresh new territory for her missionary work.

It didn't take long for Mother to discover how many of the

children who had become my new playmates had parents who had not been saved. She could not understand how mortified and angry I felt when she took it upon herself to tell our Jewish neighbors that they were going to hell because they had not accepted Jesus as their savior. Also on our block was a family's children with whom I was forbidden to play. Mother had found out that their father owned a liquor store. Mother took the first opportunity to ring our neighbor's doorbell to inform the family that if they did not become fundamentalists they were going to hell, and especially, their father was going to hell anyway because he was selling spirits of the "devil."

BEING IN ONE'S RIGHT MIND

Christian fundamentalists believe awareness of the truth equates to "being in one's right mind." The idea that belief in the Christian fundamentalist doctrine was regarded as "being in one's right mind" then justified accusation of the non-believer as being possessed by demons, being mentally unstable, or perhaps addicted to evil substances, such as alcohol. Needless to say, not only were we not a big hit in the new neighborhood, but moving to this new area of the city once and for all separated us from the friends we had once had in the old neighborhood and with whom my parents had socialized before they became fundamentalists. We had even less opportunity to ever see these friends again and eventually lost touch entirely. This distancing was mutual, as our old friends did not particularly relish spending their time fending off our aggressive Christian missionary work. For my brother and me, our challenge soon became looking for new friends whom our mother had not alienated and keeping those who were "unsaved" far away from her sincere but lethal Christian love.

From the start, I didn't share my mother's judgment that only the people who did things our way had a fair crack at heaven. But, on the other hand, I was never convinced that I could ever be good enough to ensure my own salvation, either. While my first trip down the aisle to the admission and baptismal cleansing of my sins had been sold to me as a one-time-only affair, I soon came to realize that making a new confession of my sins was to be on-going. As a child I would dread our church's yearly Revival, when visiting evangelists preached on the subject of "Hell, Fire, and Damnation." Using theatrics, they would terrify me by proclaiming, "The wages of sin are death." In fact, fear of hell is one of my most pervasive memories. There was a lot of fear within the church, mainly because the fear of spending eternity in a fiery hell, the fear of sinning in act or thought, and the fear of Satan.

Ministers always described the punishment of hell by presenting vivid descriptions of this place of torture. Satan is forever a threat to the Christian fundamentalist, who is taught that this clever, wily, and evil devil roams the world and constantly plots to trick Christian fundamentalists. The Bible warns,

> *Be sober, be vigilant; because your adversary the devil,*
> *as a roaring lion, walketh about, seeking whom he may devour.*
> II PETER (5:8)

The message is straightforward: anyone who does not believe in Christian fundamentalism will be eternally damned to hell. Life on earth may be prosperous for the unbeliever, but after death, he or she will suffer an incomprehensible punishment.

I had a terrible fear of going to hell. The whole church service was geared toward making us feel terrible about our sins. And it wasn't hard for me to find new ones to repent. Sometimes I was afraid I was going to go to hell simply because of the fact that I was afraid. Somehow it meant that I didn't trust Jesus enough. Other times, I thought that I was going to go straight to hell because I was mad at how hard the minister was working at getting us to feel the fear. When I got a little older, and noticed that there was a contradiction in the Bible's messaging about the whole fear thing, I felt doomed by my inner questioning about this, as well.

INCREASING AWARENESS

In fact, as the years passed, I became increasingly aware of the fact that there are lots of contradictions and mixed messages in the Bible, not to mention hypocrisy in the body of Christ, itself. I began to realize that contradictions had started cropping up everywhere I turned. Children in Christian fundamentalist homes are promised that God is loving. Yet they are presented over and over again with the threat of a punishing, vindictive, angry and vengeful God. They are taught that they are created in the image of God but that self-love is the sin of pride and cause for damnation. They are told to love their neighbors, but accept that these others will burn in hell forever if they do not convert. They are admonished to love their parents, but are expected to turn against their family if necessary to serve the church. Hypocrisy and mixed messages abound as the individual who raises her voice to question or protest quickly finds herself labeled disloyal.

Not only were the teachings laden with contradictions and mixed messages, but in fact, my inquiring mind could not help but notice that there were interpretations of Biblical passages that seemed to me to take a whole lot of liberty with the material—and some that seemed to have no connection to the Bible whatsoever. I remember wondering why there weren't any African-Americans in our church, for example. I scanned the Bible for the reason but could find no explanation. I remember asking my mother about this curious absence. My mother's immediate response, a faithful repetition of the minister's own thoughts on the subject, was: "They don't want to be with us. They want to be in their own churches!"

INTERPRETATION

Our minister, like all of the fundamentalist ministers who came to visit, reserved the right to "interpret" (as in meaning "to justify") any contradictions, obscure and difficult passages, or alleged discrepancies in the Bible. Cultural biases and racist thinking freely played out in our Sunday school classrooms, from the pulpit and even in casual conversation, such as that between a mother and her daughter about the absence of African-Americans at our church. Our minister was greatly influenced by a particular interpretative Bible called the Scofield Reference Bible. Biased is a more appropriate adjective, as Scofield sold his personal interpretations of the most popular version of the Bible, The King James Version, as God's own truth. He picked and chose selectively from both the Old and New Testaments, applying the creativity of his own imagination to alternately ignore or emphasize certain Biblical passages to prove his points. Following Scofield, our minister read scripture in such a way as to predict the end of time. He foretold of Christ's second coming, a time when Christians will be caught up into the heavens to meet Jesus. Metaphor was translated into irrefutable fact, as faithful readers of the Scofield Bible orient themselves toward the cataclysmic event referred to as "the Rapture." My mother memorized this passage, viewing it through Scofield's eyes:

For the Lord himself shall descend from heaven with a shout, with the voice of the archangel, and with the trump of God: and the dead in Christ shall rise first.
I THESSALONIANS (4:16–17)

These were powerful words that had a profound effect on my family. I remember one occasion in particular, when I was about 12 years old. I was inside the house with my mother, and my father was working in the garden in the back yard. It was a balmy spring day, one of those happy moments when we were all at home rather than at church. I was practicing piano. My brother was in his bedroom coloring. Mother was studying her Bible. Rapt in my music, I didn't pay any attention when Mother went outside to call my father in for lunch. The next thing I heard was Mother's high-pitched scream! I rushed outside and found her frozen in horror. "Mother! What's wrong!" I cried out. She could barely reply: "It's your father. He's gone!" "Gone?" My mind raced over the horrible possibilities, bracing myself for tragedy. But before I could contemplate any specifics, mother continued: "The Rapture has happened and your father has been taken up to the clouds, but I have been left behind!" Just then, my father came around the corner of the house, where he'd been pruning my beloved gardenias. She threw herself into his arms, as relieved that she had not missed the Rapture as I was that my father was still alive.

DEAD SERIOUS

In retrospect, this story may sound amusing. But in our family's reality, hell, the second coming, rapture, were all deadly serious. And the ramifications, as profound as they were in terms of how our family operated on a day-to-day basis, are even more sobering when you multiply our experiences by the millions of other people who think similarly. As I will discuss more thoroughly in a later chapter, the idea of the second coming of Christ and the various events interpreted to happen before, during and after, has greatly determined the politics of the Christian Right. Influencing politicians at all levels of government, all the way to the top, many of our leaders' decisions are impacted, directly or indirectly, by those whose motivation is to accelerate the advent of the second coming.

I did not drown during my baptism. But neither did I escape. The minister pinched my nose tight and held on to me with a firmness of grip I knew I had not the power to defy. In fact, my baptism as a ten-year-old was not dissimilar to the hold Christian fundamentalism had on me throughout my childhood, teens and well into my twenties. The effect of the teachings of my religion piled up on me, layer upon layer, in effect closing off all my escape routes. How, then, did I ever find a way out? Here, after all, I sit writing this as a woman who has her doctorate in The Philosophy of Human Science from a leading, secular academic institution. I avoid fundamentalist churches and culture and I play cards and dance from time to time. But of all the freedoms I now enjoy, the greatest gift is the reclamation of the long-lost spirit of the happy nine-year-old girl I once was and the knowledge that I am, indeed, good enough and that God loves my authentic self just the way I am. This is the spirit that I have come to think of as "Healing Eve." In the next chapter, and throughout the remainder of this book, I describe how I—and many others—have found freedom from fundamentalism. For me, the first crack of light appeared when I crossed the threshold from early childhood into my teenaged years. It seems that when my religion laid plans to cut off all possible escape routes, it neglected to take one thing into consideration: the power of hormones on the teenaged spirit.

CHAPTER TWO

Reclaiming My Authentic Self

Throughout my childhood, I believed in the promise of the Christian fundamentalism within which I was raised. Even while I struggled to overcome the conviction of my own sinfulness, born of Eve's sin in the Garden of Eden, I bought the notion that the only hope for happiness—in this life and the next—was within the church. Accept without questioning absolute truth as taught by the church, follow the rigid rules of conduct and keep quiet about contradictions, mixed messages and hypocrisy, and I would be guaranteed the fruits of the spirit. Of course, the flipside of the promise was what really grabbed my attention: be less than perfect in any of this, and I was headed straight to an eternity in hell. It was many years before I could revisit the memories of my painful childhood in the fundamentalist church community with any sense of perspective. In fact, only by viewing my life through the eyes of the cultural anthropologist I have since become, could I finally bring any objectivity at all to my early life experiences.

As it turns out, the transition from childhood to adolescence— including the hard-won escape I share with you in this chapter— followed a general pattern that social scientists consider to be "normal" in modern society. The women in my study who had broken free from a wide variety of toxic versions of fundamentalist beliefs and communities followed similar psychosocial patterns on their way to spiritual freedom. Inspired by this model, as taught to me by my doctoral mentor at Saybrook Graduate School, Dr. Stanley Krippner, I formulated the three-stage Healing Eve Process I share in this book.

Among the many adaptations of the personal mythology model to the particular case of women working to reclaim their authentic selves from the toxic layers of fundamentalism, I can tell you both from social observation and from first-hand experience that the process feels anything but normal. In fact, from my anthropological studies, I recognized that women inside of fundamentalism share more in common with pre-modern, "tribal" communities in one important respect, than with most aspects of contemporary American society. The one respect is this. Like the primitive cultures I studied while pursuing my first graduate degree in anthropology, fundamentalists share a unified view of the world. This view is airtight, shunning or marginalizing any perspective that might challenge the group's sense of ultimate truth and meaning. Exclusivity creates a climate in which any view that is different from the fundamentalist belief is a serious threat and is very dangerous to the believer. As an example, in Christian fundamentalism, with the exception of missionary outreach, adherents are encouraged to associate exclusively with believers and to avoid nonbelievers.

A scripture verse used to uphold this belief is:

Be ye not unequally yoked together with unbelievers:
for what fellowship hath righteousness with unrighteousness?
And what communion hath light with darkness?
II CORINTHIANS (6:14)

Most people in modern society, outside of fundamentalist cultures, are far more likely to be exposed to and influenced by multiple points of view. "Normal" people faced with external challenges to their original belief systems process inner and external conflicts in a sensible way and get on with their lives. For the fundamentalist, both the promise of the original belief system and the flip-side threat should one stray from the group mind are much more extreme. While women breaking free from fundamentalism experience a struggle so intense that it challenges the very definition of "normal" development, my research reveals through the life stories of the women shared in this book that ultimate success is possible—even for us. By negotiating the programmed, reactive and wisdom stages of the healing process, any one of us can make up for lost developmental time to live a "normal enough" life: one full of joy, freedom and authenticity. Throughout the remainder of this book, our stories illustrate how the steps of the healing process played out in our lives—sometimes intentionally, sometimes by accident or, dare I say it, sometimes from luck.

ONE: THE PROGRAMMED STAGE

In the last chapter, I described my childhood in fundamentalism, exposing the toxic layers of the original promises and their flip-side threats. Following a "literal" interpretation of the Bible, my culture encouraged its daughters to surrender our own thoughts and feelings in order to guess what was being asked of us.

Earlier I mentioned that my family picked up a phrase, "What Would Jesus Do?" for every decision to be made. Even today, the letters "WWJD?" appear as a slogan on coffee mugs, T-shirts, visors, and bumper stickers to remind the Christian fundamentalist to consider, "What Would Jesus Do?" whenever a decision is to be made. Our family's confidence in our own judgment was replaced with feelings of inadequacy. For Christian fundamentalists, decision-making is a daunting task, for they believe that there is only one correct and right choice and that the consequences of making the "wrong" decision could mean eternal punishment.

For young girls growing into adolescence, foremost among the rigid rules of conduct was the one related to sex. Don't. No premarital sex acts, certainly. But no sexual thoughts or impulses, either. Christian fundamentalism treats emotions as morally equivalent to behavior. Biblical commandments exhort believers to love, to refrain from fear, and to refrain from anger, as though believers could control these feelings.

> *But now ye also put off all these; anger, wrath, malice, blasphemy, filthy communication out of your mouth.*
> COLOSSIANS (3:8)

Note that in the above verse, anger, wrath, and malice are listed as though they are behaviors, like blasphemy and filthy communication. Anger is conceived to be the equivalent of murder. And if an adolescent girl experiences lustful feelings, this is the same as committing a defiled sexual act. This is no minor infraction. Fornication or voluntary sexual relations between unmarried individuals is prohibited at least 36 times in the Bible.

In order to avoid going to hell, adolescent girls were actively taught to make every attempt to deny normal, healthy sexual impulses. They were, in essence, required to hide their authentic selves. Years later, many of the women in my research group have still had to work with professional counselors in order to learn how to deal with these long-denied feelings. Others expended a great deal of energy doing inner work, such as art therapy, journaling, and workshops.

While I, too, have struggled with these issues all of my life, at the time I believed that I had found a loophole. For when it came to sex, the rigid rules of conduct allowed one permissible outlet: marriage to the right boy. If I were to marry young, I could "own" my sexuality while at the same time, avoiding the fiery pits of hell.

OUTSIDE INFLUENCES

The fundamentalist promise of good girls garnering the fruits of the spirit collided with an unexpected outside influence: television. Watching American Bandstand with friends in our new home, I banked on the promise that some day my prince would come. Even if we couldn't dance ourselves, my best friend and I became entranced by the young couples who danced for us every afternoon under the tutelage of our benevolent ringleader: Dick Clark. For us, the television screen became a portal to a world beyond the boundaries of Christian fundamentalism: a world where people our age could dance freely with one another and relate to each other with an authenticity and passion that gave us goose bumps! Even when we couldn't be together, my girlfriend and I would turn on the television, call each other on the telephone and discuss what each girl on the show was wearing. But the appeal of the show was much more than about the clothes the girls were wearing. While we didn't have the words to express it then, we had stumbled onto a worldview far more appealing than the one that had previously conscribed our rigid reality.

These precious afternoons came so early in the history of television, the church community was unaware of their influence on us. Viewing our new role models through a breach in the rigid rules of conduct that ordered our lives, we worked hard to dress exactly like the dancers we so admired: a felt skirt with "crinoline" petticoats, which my friend and I starched in the bathtub to make them stiff, a pageboy, fuzzy sweaters with changeable collars and suede loafers with the customary penny in them.

Our early forays into the world of fashion had a deeper purpose, of course. I was out to catch the right boy. What was our community's definition of the right boy? He need fulfill only one criteria: be a Christian fundamentalist from a "good," church going family. Nothing else mattered: not that he may have an uncontrollable temper, be spoiled or be motivated by materialistic rather than spiritual goals.

When I started dating in my mid-teens, I knew what the rules were and what was expected of me. I had one date with a wonderful young man, but when we got to the subject of religion, he told me he was a Catholic. I did not go out with him anymore, and when my parents heard the reason, they praised me for adhering to the "scriptures." Soon thereafter, I began dating an "acceptable" alternative: a member of our church. In fact, as early as our first date, my parents had already planned that I would marry him, have lots of kids, belong to the Southern Baptist Church, do church work, and become pillars of the community! Wedding plans were already on the table when I met somebody else: the man who was to become my first husband, at a party. I was only 17.

The assumption that "my prince had come" was only an illusion. While Perry was from the right part of town, he was a non-denominational liberal who had the misfortune of having fallen head over heels in love with a fundamentalist. I loved the attention—and the challenge of it. In fact, in retrospect, Perry may well have been my first, albeit unconscious, act of rebellion. The truth is that with Perry, I had found another loophole. In Perry's case, even if I knew deep down that he wasn't "one of us," he was willing to act the part. Dutifully, Perry accompanied me to church every Sunday and listened to me quote Bible verses to him ad nauseam. My parents tried to break us up, fearing what turned out to be the truth: that Perry was, in fact, an "outside influence" who would ultimately burst their dreams of grandchildren raised faithfully within the church. Nevertheless, as Perry continued to abide by the letter of the law, we continued to date. By the time I went off to attend Baylor University we were engaged, and he was waiting for me fresh-faced and eager at the altar of my parents' church when I dropped out of college at the age of 19 to marry him.

A "CAREER"

Despite my father's disappointment in my decision to deprive myself of an education, this was—to my way of thinking—no great loss. Even at Baylor, it had soon become clear that the only majors that I could pursue were those that were acceptable to the church: nurturing roles especially suited for women, such as nursing, music or education. The choice of a major is restricted since a woman's real "career" is expected to be church work and caring for her family. I certainly could not aspire to male-oriented positions within the church or in the workplace. I chose nursing...a career that had absolutely nothing to do with my authentic aspirations, preferences or even interests.

Until the day our wedding was over, my husband conformed to the dictates of my church, abiding by every Christian fundamentalist detail regarding the ceremony. His parents had no say in the planning of the wedding. It had to be in my church, and while my husband's parents would have preferred that the reception take place at their country club, this, too, took place in the bosom of my church community. His parents gave us a brand new Volkswagen, and after the honeymoon, we moved to Colorado, where Perry finished his degree in commercial art.

Our marriage was flawed from the beginning because of our immature thinking that we would live "happily ever after." It did solve the problem of pre-marital sex; but the rush to the altar did not give us time to assess each other's differences as they pertained to personality traits, ambitions, or lifetime goals. As we were finding out, it would take a lot to bridge that gap. While trying to work through our differences, I escaped into a timely opportunity: a job as an office assistant at a large oil company. Perry liked that I had taken the job, as it brought income into our little family—and took financial pressure off of him. As I went along, I slowly acquired more secretarial skills in night classes and moved up the ladder as the secretary to the vice president of the company.

During this period, I met the wife of the owner of the company, an elegant woman, as sure of her place in the world as I was unsure of my own. I daydreamed about becoming somebody like her someday. She was so confident in herself and her abilities! Studying her, I made a list of her attributes and decided to begin emulating them, one by one. One of my first steps was to enroll in a modeling school, which held classes on etiquette, dress and poise. Meeting people outside of my fundamentalist community at work and at school, I began taking some risks: putting myself in charge of my life and taking pride in myself. If I had stopped to think about it, I would have realized that what I was doing could well have been considered to be sins. But away from the eyes of my church community, I had somehow managed to "bracket" self-judgment long enough to take my first baby steps in the direction of liberation from fundamentalism. Three months before Perry graduated, my company decided to close its Colorado operation and consolidate its operations in Houston. I was offered a temporary position in Houston to help facilitate the move. I would have to leave Perry in Colorado and move alone, even if only on a temporary basis, to another state. For the first time in my life, instead of thinking *What Would Jesus Do?* I found myself asking *"What Would Jimmy Do?"* What Jimmy would do was scandalize her husband, their families and the church community by venturing off on her own—without his permission—on this assignment.

WHAT WOULD JIMMY DO?

During this three-month assignment, I relished being in the company of these people, all of whom were in some kind of transition. As a part of this new community, I got my first glimpse of what a sheltered life I had lived. At assignment's end, I was a different person who joined my husband who had, in the meanwhile, moved back to our home town. Everybody was waiting for me, my father having been instrumental in arranging a new position for Perry. Falling back into the family and church womb, I was 24 years old when I had my first and only child, a boy. My parents and I doted on my son and despite their disappointment with my husband's refusal to accompany me to church, they still had visions of my glorious future as a leader of women doing missionary outreach to nonbelievers. Fate once again intervened, however, in the form of Perry's job transfer to Southern California. As soon as we got to Los Angeles, I sought out the Baptist Church, searching for clarity and understanding and unbeknownst to me at the time, giving not only my marriage but the church one last chance. It was the only place I could think of to go for solace. Questioning my marriage didn't sit well with the members of my California church and I soon realized it would not have gone any better back at my home church, either. Christian fundamentalism, wherever it was located, could not embrace us in our pain because we had broken one of the rigid rules of behavior. Marital discord was a threat to the church's own self-image, and so it was easier for the members to declare a divorce "unbiblical" than to extend compassion to the young mother sobbing out her grief before them.

I was not the only one whose cries for help went unheard. During my childhood I experienced many examples in my church of unhappily married couples, most of whom, like me, had married too young to know better. Now, they were doomed to being bound together for the rest of their lives. Even as a young child, I could not help but realize that following the scripture to the letter did not, in fact, bring forth a joyful Christian! Those couples in our church, who, indeed, got a divorce anyway were immediately ostracized, and even if it had been possible for them to stay, it was not worth the pain of remaining in the church after the divorce took place. Prominent couples—including deacons, Sunday school teachers and choir directors—would suddenly be gone. I remember one incident, in particular. A staff member had an affair with his secretary. The two disappeared, but their fall from grace, as well as their subsequent divorces from their spouses, was made public in the form of humiliating Sunday school lessons and minister's sermons.

I turned to the church for comfort and understanding in regard to my unhappy marriage. But where was the community's, not to mention God's unconditional love now? The pain was made that much worse because the promise is so much greater. In fact, one of the first Bible scriptures we are taught in Christian fundamentalism is the following verse:

God is love.

1 JOHN (4:16)

If one hears that God is love, one believes that it is an all-consuming, unconditional type of love that one can always count on. Christian fundamentalism promises believers a powerful experience through the outpouring of God's love for the individual, and the reciprocal love of the believer, as well as in the association with other loving believers. Evidence of God's love is God sending his son to die as a sacrifice for the sins of all humans, by God's mercy and goodness toward all believers. In the Holy Bible: Authorized King James Version (1976) the publishers include a topical concordance. In this concordance, there are 162 Bible verses listed that relate to God's mercy, goodness, and love. In the Old Testament book of Psalms alone, there are 24 verses that refer to the adoration of God and God's goodness and mercy. Numerous verses exhort believers to love one another, and the expression "Christian love" is frequently used by Christian fundamentalists to refer to non-erotic affection and caring.

ANGRY GOD

Ironically, the foremost reason given for the disillusionment with Christian fundamentalism in my study of women centered on the lack of love in their relationships to God, the church, community, family, and self. No one in my study reported experiencing positive emotional well-being in relation to their fundamentalist upbringings. In fact, over and over again, the women in my study reported a portrait of a vindictive, angry, and vengeful God. Unwittingly, we had accepted the notion that Eve had, on our behalf, taken on God's wrath for the sake of that forbidden fruit. Not only were the men in our lives granted power over us, in order to keep our wickedness in line, but so were we doomed to an angry God, forever punishing us for Eve's disobedience. Few of the participants reported experiencing a loving God until long after they left Christian fundamentalism.

From the time I'd first left home, I'd been becoming more and more aware of my authentic self crying out to me from the depths of my soul. However, the day I walked out of the Southern Baptist church in California—my cries for help met only by a cold and abrupt dismissal—was the day my retrieval of an authentic life began in earnest. The church had obviously broken its promise to me. Not only was there no reward as a fruit of the spirit, compensating me for a lifeline struggle to be good enough, but neither was there a church community to offer me solace and understanding, when my dreams fell to ash.

HEALING BEGINS

Years later, while studying for my doctorate, I recognized this moment as the successful negotiation of the programmed stage of the Healing Eve Process. The programmed stage is based on the understanding that all human beings are raised within society, training them from birth to view the world through a particular emotional lens. Our parents are our first teachers, defining for us what it means to be good or bad; what our "world" is and how are we to relate to it. Schools, media and churches are other major sources of definition, although there are literally hundreds of thousands of impressions made upon each one of us every day of our lives—from the billboards we pass on our road trips to the food our society considers desirable to eat. All contribute to our sense of reality. For fundamentalists, the religious community plays a particularly potent role. Children born or raised within fundamentalism are taught from an early age to believe that the community's idea of how the world works is the only valid truth.

Drs. Feinstein and Krippner point out that, "people often live their lives with very little awareness of the lens through which they are looking." But while this may be as true of individuals raised within liberal (or no) religion as it is of fundamentalists, fundamentalists have an added burden: the admonition that anything not within or authorized by their closed society's view of the world is forbidden.

The nearly super-human work of the individual traversing the first stage of the process of Healing Eve includes becoming aware that the promises and threats of the beliefs with which they were raised are not the only reality—but merely one particularly toxic view of reality. In fundamentalism, the term "worldview" best describes the encompassing model by which human beings experience their lives as having meaning. Some social scientists, such as Dr. Krippner, call this "myth." In the case of fundamentalism, the worldview is communicated, in part, through a series of promises. The woman's soul becomes buried under layers and layers of toxic beliefs, assumptions and threats. Fundamentalism packs a particularly potent punch to our original programming. There is great testimony to the divine spark within each of us. I saw it in so many of the women I interviewed. All raised within fundamentalism, they came to realize that their authentic selves had the right to be retrieved—against all odds.

THE COMFORT OF COMMUNITY

There was no love in the church where I had sought refuge. But I did find comfort, community and support for my awakening in the most unlikely place: a women's lounge in downtown Los Angeles where I had once again taken up my secretarial career. The building I worked in was one of the older buildings, made solidly of stone. I remember the elevator operator, a proper gentleman wearing white gloves, who shuttled us efficiently among the seven floors. On the second floor was a women's lounge, where most of us on a budget brought our lunches everyday.

Among my friends was a striking receptionist from another company in the building. For some reason she just assumed that I was "religious," probably because I had moved to California from the "Bible Belt." In any case, she sought me out for advice concerning the possibility of becoming engaged to a wonderful young man who worked in the next office. "What would happen if we got married and then I changed my mind?" Without missing a beat, a Bible verse came pouring out of me:

Whosoever putteth away his wife, and marrieth another, committeth adultery: and whosoever marrieth her that is put away from her husband committeth adultery.

LUKE (16:18)

I was just as astounded at my blurting out this Bible verse as she was! But, the most profound revelation came to me later that day when I realized that I didn't really believe in what Luke proclaimed anymore, and that I, indeed, was the one who was thinking about a divorce! From that moment on, there was no turning back. The day that I sobbed out my woes before a gathering of unsympathetic pillars of the church was the last time I ever again entered a fundamentalist church as a believer. However personally momentous was my decision to leave the church, my experience was consistent with the findings of my research: rarely, if ever, is the break experienced by the woman, herself, as a celebration. In fact, she may well dread the thought that by defying the tribal consciousness of her birthright, she has doomed herself to a life as an outsider. In fact, she is likely to carry with her the possibility that the fundamentalists may be right, after all, and that by reclaiming her authentic existence, she may have destined herself to an eternity in hell. While I cared deeply about my parents—and I certainly worried about what impact my newfound independence might be having on my afterlife—I had become willing to take on hell itself in order to own, express and act upon my true feelings. I had successfully negotiated the first stage's task: acute awareness of the inadequacy of the worldview within which I was raised, and the search for something better. At this point, I entered the second reactive stage of the process leading to the healing of Eve.

TWO: THE REACTIVE STAGE

For the fundamentalist woman, awakening comes later rather than sooner in life. Most of the women I interviewed were way down the road before they realized that the promises of their fundamentalist worldview would not be kept. They were in abusive marriages. Trapped in unfulfilling educational paths or jobs. Putting off having children for fear of perpetuating their unhappiness in the next generation and any one of a hundred variations on the theme of the ravages of fundamentalism's broken promises. Not surprisingly, disillusionment for the fundamentalist woman carries with it intense negative feelings of rebellion, anger and sadness. Pain accompanies the authentic self's first exposure to the bright light of day. One mourns the sacrifices one has been asked to make, the lost time and opportunities not to mention out and out mistakes.

You wonder if you've really got what it will take to stand up to all the toxic forces that have been acting upon you. You fear whether you are taking risks that will actually pay off in anything other than a lifetime of even greater regret. At the same time, this stage is rich with experimentation. There must be other, better ways to live our lives and relate to the universe, divine and mundane. Again, the divine spark urges the woman breaking free from fundamentalism to journey through the void of disillusionment toward a new and healthier life. The toxic layers become visible— exposed and therefore, at last, vulnerable to critique, revision and removal. In reaction to the illusory promises of her past, the healing woman responds to, creates and avoids various options: sometimes making mistakes, other times stumbling onto new, healthier possibilities. Often she acts out of anger reactively to that from which she is emerging. Sometimes she transcends her past and tries something completely new.

BRANCHING OUT

I became more and more disillusioned with Christian fundamentalism as I began working with people of various nationalities, sexual orientations, races and belief systems. I could not see how these people were "bad," doomed to an eternity in hell because of their non-belief in Christian fundamentalism. Among my new friends were several who had also been raised in authoritarian or oppressive religious communities. They weren't just Christian fundamentalists, either. This was when I first began to realize that there are orthodoxies in many religions that burden people with beliefs that no longer serve them. One friend in particular shared with me her most astonishing decision: she had chosen to leave her childhood religious upbringing behind—just like that! What a concept—she actually believed she had a choice in her future! She actually felt she could be "selfish" enough to make life choices that made her life more fulfilling!

I, too, became eager to experiment with new ways of relating to the world. Among my new friends were people who had been subjected to the church's racism and bigotry: African-Americans and homosexuals. You may recall from the previous chapter that my minister expressed his own negative views of these as well as other minorities, implying that the judgments he passed were not his own personal bias, but to be accepted as "gospel." Since our minister had told us that African-Americans would rather attend their own churches and that was the reason there were none in our membership, I had only been exposed to African-Americans in service positions, or an occasional missionary from abroad who would be invited to visit our church. Aside from these contacts, the greater church community heartily embraced segregation as Biblically based. As a child, when I went to a public swimming pool, there were signs posted to indicate which pools were for the Whites and which pools were for the Blacks. Our public water fountains also had designations for the use of Blacks or Whites.

This part of the fundamentalist worldview began unraveling for me almost the moment I left home the first time with my husband. Soon after the beginning of Perry's first term at the university in Colorado, I was invited to a meeting of "wives" of students. When I entered the room, the first thing I noticed was that there were a number of African-American women, sipping glasses of wine and wearing outfits every bit as chic as my own. Realizing that many of these women had more education than I, the childhood bias lifted instantaneously, and by the time I had joined the lunchroom clique in Los Angeles, I drew no distinction between races when selecting my friends.

Homosexuality carried with it an even more overt bias within the fundamentalist community, as the gay individual was routinely referred to by our minister as an "abomination" to the Lord. When I was a young girl I really didn't know the term homosexual, but I knew that when there was going to be a family reunion, many members of the family refused to come if a distant cousin of mother's attended. He was a "queer." The distant cousin decided not to attend. When I made friends with homosexuals later in life, I can still remember the voice of my mother reminding me that homosexuality was not acceptable to God and that it was my obligation to let them know that unless they shaped up, they were heading straight to hell! Of course I didn't, learning, instead, to judge people on the basis of their characters and values, rather than on color or sexual orientation.

Many of my new friends were seekers and intellectuals, who introduced me to books like Ayn Rand's *The Fountainhead*, Maxwell Maltz's *Psycho-Cybernetics* and the very first "unauthorized" book I read cover to cover: *The Power of Positive Thinking* by Dr. Norman Vincent Peale. This certainly was not a new book, having been written in 1956, but of course I had never come in contact with it. The idea of positive thinking written by a minister didn't compute in my world of compliant conduct and mortal threats, but I was intrigued and decided to look at it. Well, it was an eye opener for me. Peale, a Protestant minister, had somehow combined the Bible with psychology to reveal the inherent goodness of human beings, rather than the fundamentalist conviction of their inherent sinfulness. Furthermore, Dr. Peale asserted that since God loves us, we had His blessing to use the power of our minds to find peace and harmony. The idea that we could visualize with our minds solutions to our problems and then attain what we visualized was a radical departure from the dogma of my childhood religion. "Believe in Yourself"; "How to Create Your Own Happiness"; "Power to Solve Personal Problems"—even the chapter titles gave the responsibility to have a say in the direction of one's life to the individual. The very notion of selfishness was turned upside down, with pride and self-esteem the path to God rather than to hell. I couldn't put the book down.

FORBIDDEN PHILOSOPHY

Not long thereafter, a friend asked me if I enjoyed the Ayn Rand books. I checked *The Fountainhead* out of the library, encountering Ayn's universe of strong, self-motivated people. Her philosophy of "objectivism" proposes that the moral purpose of being human is his or her own happiness. Productive achievement is a human being's most noble activity, and reason is the only absolute. In her book, *Atlas Shrugged*, one of her characters defined pride as thoughts held by persons that are their own highest value. Pride, like all of man's values, has to be earned through the creation of one's own character. Ayn Rand's philosophy was so radical it took my breath away. I saw her books as extreme, rejecting her atheism but admiring the self-sufficiency of her characters.

Another book that had a tremendous affect on my life was Dr. Maxwell Maltz's book, *Psycho-Cybernetics*. Dr. Maltz's premise was that people have inaccurate perceptions of themselves, often distorted by unchallenged and often erroneous beliefs embedded in the subconscious mind. Dr. Maltz asserted that "positive thinking" can only work well in conjunction with a positive self-image. Like Dr. Peale, Dr. Maltz offered his assumption about God's belief in human beings. He asserted, that "Fundamentalists tell us that man's chief purpose and reason for living is to 'glorify God' and the Humanists tell us that man's primary purpose is to 'express himself fully'. However, if we take the premise that God is a loving Creator and has the same interest in his Creation that an earthly father has in his children, then it seems to me that the Fundamentalists and the Humanists are saying the same thing."

Unlike Rand, Maltz and Peale did not throw out the concept of God or a Creator. Rather, they threw out the concept of the "unworthy, sinful human being," and suddenly, the concept of a God rooting for the success and happiness of every human being was an exciting possibility. The added bonus was that each human being had the power to create her own "heaven" on earth.

I had already practiced the development of a positive self-image back in Colorado, when I made a list of attributes exemplified by the sophisticated wife of my first boss. Now I began to visualize the kind of marriage I wanted, the life I hoped to live. My present marriage did not satisfy any of my aspirations. By then, Perry had lost his job, and his introversion held him back from actively seeking employment. This was the final straw, and I filed for divorce. Once again our parents attempted to come to the rescue. With or without Perry, my parents pressured me to come back home with my son, and Perry's parents offered me a blank check to change my mind. I know not the source of my strength. But I stood up to the pressures and temptations on all sides and using my half of our tax rebate check, moved my son and myself into an apartment, bought my first used car and found myself a new job.

This was, in retrospect, a self-chosen crisis. Out of my disillusionment, a voice that had been whispering to me for years was finally loud enough to out-shout my minister. *I am not crazy. I am not a sinner. I am not Eve. I have the right to my own thoughts and feelings. I have the right to protect myself from abuse and I have the right to judge others by my own criteria.* At the age of 27, I officially turned my back on the Christian fundamentalist community, and threw myself into the task of creating my own, authentic life. I had now negotiated the second stage, the stage of reactivity to my original programmed beliefs, and had entered into the final "Wisdom Stage" of the Healing Eve Process.

THREE: THE WISDOM STAGE

In the first programmed stage, the seeker of healing becomes aware of and then uncomfortable with the question: "What can I do to make God happy with me?" As she moves into the second stage, the question became: "How can I do this better than the way I was raised?" In the third stage, the stage of wisdom, I discovered a revolutionary, new question: "What do I want?"

Resolution takes the woman beyond reacting to the broken promises of her upbringing to a place where she can finally make peace with her past. In this third and final stage, she receives the benefit of a new promise: trust in herself that she can utilize her own growing bank of skills in order to make better decisions. It is not that she won't still make mistakes from time-to-time—still feel sadness over the lost opportunities for a happy childhood and an easier life—but she now values her authenticity above all else. Becoming more secure in her own internal processes, she finds herself able to retrieve aspects of value from her past and integrate them into her new beliefs. Only when she can stop reacting to her past does she attain true liberation of body, mind and spirit.

In a later chapter, I will once again take up the story of my life to describe what making peace with fundamentalism has turned out to look like for me. Suffice it to say that authenticity came slowly. Bit by bit, I eliminated the principles of absolute truth, rigid rules of conduct in my life, and worked on healing the emotional mixed messages. I made many brave choices (and a few foolish ones).

Eventually I negotiated the void of reactivity to come to a place in which I feel embraced by a loving and forgiving universe.

Just around the time I left Perry, I went to work for a wonderful man who has since become the husband for whom I longed. We raised our son free of fundamentalism. Overcoming my ingrained feelings of unworthiness, I started on an educational tract that veered sharply from the nursing major from which I fled. Starting with a license in real estate, I moved on to a B.A. and M.A. in anthropology. Ultimately I received my Ph.D. in Philosophy of Human Science from Saybrook Research and Graduate School, and I now have a new career as an author and teacher.

A NEW PROMISE TO MYSELF

While I have kept my own promise to myself, never to enter a fundamentalist church again as a believer, I have found that I have reclaimed the core of moral values I was given as a child. On occasion, I will turn to a familiar scripture for comfort—although you would be far more likely to find me meditating or journaling, utilizing any one of a number of spiritual or psychological disciplines I have picked up along the way while healing Eve. I never stopped loving my parents, although I disagreed with their religious convictions and rigid rules of conduct until the days each of them passed away. Most of all, I have savored the reclamation of "WWJD" to mean "What Would Jimmy Do?" and trust that as long as I am faithful to the divine spark within, that what I do will always be good enough. I no longer fear that if I make a mistake, I will be ostracized, unforgiven and doomed to hell. For anyone raised in the fundamentalist environment, you will recognize how huge an accomplishment this is!

It's time, now, to turn to the stories of a number of the women I met on our journeys to healing Eve. Coming from a wide variety of fundamentalist formulations, our stories weave together through the themes I have introduced in these first chapters, supporting and enriching both our personal and our mutual discoveries.

CHAPTER THREE

One Trunk, Many Branches

For the Jews, Mohammedans and Christians among others,
man is master by divine right, the fear of God will therefore
repress any impulse towards revolt in the downtrodden female.

SIMONE DE BEAUVOIR

W e were eight strangers, seated together by chance around the dinner table at a gathering of professional women interested in women's rights. In turn, we were to introduce ourselves and to say a few words about our careers. I decided that my work researching women who have broken free from Protestant fundamentalism would be of more interest to this particular audience than my work in real estate. I was not even half-way through my already short introduction when one of the women challenged me. "Why just Protestant fundamentalism? Why not Catholicism?" We never did get to hear what Rachel does for a living (later on, I found out that she is an executive in the banking business.) Instead, Rachel used her precious networking time to tell us about her hard-won escape from a conservative form of Catholicism. In fact, the introductions around the table could only resume after I promised to set an interview time with her, to get her full story.

This was just one variation of an experience repeated numerous times over the course of my research. Carefully, I would explain to each non-Protestant woman who approached me that I had set the parameters of my research to Protestant forms of fundamentalism as a matter of expediency. While I could not include the information non-Protestants provided as part of my formal research, it would be gratifying, indeed, to get a sense of similarities and differences experienced by women struggling to break free from other orthodoxies.

It soon became evident that many of the key findings pertaining to women raised in Protestant fundamentalism apply to women embedded in a broad spectrum of fundamentalist religions, cults and sects. There was Rachel, the former conservative Catholic, sharing with the table of strangers the pervasive fear she'd had most of her life that she might do something wrong and go to hell. In our private interview that followed, I felt like I was looking in the mirror when she explained that as she was growing up, she had been told that Catholicism was the only true religion and that her non-Catholic friends, no matter how good or loving, would never make it into heaven. I had the same uncanny experience of recognition several months later when a friend introduced me to Naomi, who identified herself as "a recovering Mormon." Naomi had grown up a youth leader in the church, eager to go on her first mission to win souls to Mormonism. When she grew into her teenaged years, she became increasingly aware of the impact of black and white thinking, rigid rules and elitism, particularly on the women in the community. These were but a few of the similarities that I uncovered as a result of meeting courageous women traveling to and from a wide variety of religious and spiritual destinations. It wasn't only the similarities that were instructive, however. Differences, too, helped illuminate the many ramifications of toxic fundamentalisms as they play out in the lives of women in a wide array of circumstances.

Following are four composite portraits based on my conversations with Catholic, Muslim, Mormon and Jewish women who have broken free from toxic institutions, communities and beliefs. Perhaps it is no accident that each of these religions, along with Protestant fundamentalism, shares a common root that includes their own particular interpretation of the story of Adam and Eve. While the storyline and theology vary from version to version, somehow it is the woman who ends up cooking and cleaning in the church kitchen (the fundamentalist Christian), relegated to the balcony at services (the orthodox Jew) or hidden behind a veil (the traditional Muslim).

FOUR PORTRAITS

Rachel's Story: A Catholic Woman's Experience Rachel was born into a conservative Catholic family, the youngest child of nine siblings. Her mother taught the girls in the family that the good Catholic woman's highest aspiration is to be a dutiful wife and mother. At the same time, Rachel was acutely aware of how exhausted her mother often was, caring for her brood with too few emotional and material resources to go around. Like many of the Protestant fundamentalists in the study, Rachel was taught early in life that Eve was responsible for bringing sin into the world: that somehow, being female was inferior to being male. This was borne out by the fact that often there seemed to be less time for the girls than the boys in her family—except when it came to enforcing the rules and meting out punishment. At home, and later on at Catholic school, it seemed to her that boys could get by with more, while the girls were being more closely watched. As a result, Rachel felt she was not really good enough for Jesus—not fully trusting that Jesus would love her no matter what.

Role models for womanhood As a result of her Catholic school education, Rachel gained two additional role models for womanhood: Mary mother of Jesus, and the nuns. From the first, she saw the nuns as being "little servants" to the priests, married to Christ but not necessarily happy. Strict disciplinarians, they inspired fear more than admiration. Then there was Mary. Mary, in Rachel's telling, had value as a female not only because she was Jesus' mother, but because of the virgin birth. Rachel was taught that out of her love and compassion, Mary could serve as a special intercessor for women. "The nuns were quick to remind us that as girls, we couldn't get to Jesus by ourselves because he is very clean and pure, while we are dirty and sinful." As hard as she tried, however, Rachel could not relate to Mary, who apparently achieved sainthood by rising above other women's biological destiny, distinguished primarily for having given virgin birth to the male savior.

Says Rachel: "As a child I followed the dictates of the nuns and priests without question, but at 13 years old, things would come up for me from the outside world that would make think, 'Wait a minute. There are other good people in the world—other worthwhile belief systems. We are not the only religion. If the nuns and priests are lying to me about one thing, what else are they lying to me about?'" In addition to her growing discontent about the secondary role of womanhood in Catholicism, she was disturbed by another aspect of the Adam and Eve creation story: the notion of original sin. She found the notion frightening and unacceptable that a newborn baby, girl or boy, is born sinful. She had been taught that unless christened, the baby would be condemned to go to a place called limbo. "I was scared to death for the babies because we were told their souls are all black."

By the time she was 16 years old, she had quit going to church. Now in her 30s, Rachel retains the idea that there is a spiritual or universal order, and she still believes in the Ten Commandments and the Golden Rule. She will now enter a church only for a special family ritual or the occasional moment of solitude.

Naomi's Story: A Mormon Woman's Experience Like Rachel, Naomi was raised in a large family, taught from her earliest memories that the only acceptable role for a Mormon woman was to be a wife and mother. "They say it's the greatest blessing of all. It is, I suppose, if that is what you want. If that's not what you want, however, it's a curse!"

As a young girl, she took church very seriously, conforming to every rule and every teaching, reading her Bible faithfully. As an adolescent, she became a leader of young adults, anticipating going on her first required "mission" to win souls to Mormonism. Through it all, she felt accepted as a woman in her church. And then, at the age of 21, she participated in an initiation that brought her closer to the inner circles of power: The Temple.

It's not that she had been previously unaware of inequalities in treatment between the sexes, but she had bought "hook, line and sinker" that this was a sign of men's reverence for women. The deeper she penetrated the institutions of power, however, the more she began to see contradictions in how the theology was actually playing out. "Men were required to revere their wives; however, men are also the priesthood and the spiritual power of the church. It is hard to separate the man as husband and the man as the spiritual power and priesthood."

Entry into heaven Naomi found it particularly disturbing when she was taught that a woman could not get into heaven unless it is through a man, either your father or your husband. Since Naomi's father had passed away, Naomi said, "It finally dawned on me, once and for all, that the only way I was going to get to the celestial realm was through marrying someone!" When she protested, she was told to shape up, or forget about going to heaven.

"The Mormon Church is big on black and white thinking: they are elitist, they are judgmental, they do not tolerate outsiders. Even though I had paid my 10% gross tithe, made a fasting offering once a month, went to Temple regularly, answered to any calling of the church, the bottom line was that I was doing all of this out of fear of what would happen to me if I didn't do it. In the end, I wouldn't have gotten to heaven anyway—not without a husband or a father in the picture."

Naomi has since left the church, seeking friendships with women and men she respects, regardless of their religious orientation. Now in her forties, and a graphics designer, she still retains her belief in a higher power, praying to God, whom she claims, "may be a Her or a He." And, she believes in miracles: the biggest miracle being, ironically, that she found her way out of Mormonism and got on with her life.

Nicky's Story: A Muslim Woman's Experience Nicky, now a successful American computer expert in her late thirties, was born in Iran to moderate Muslim parents, active participants in a liberal interpretation of the religious idea of Islam. Thriving under the reign of the Shah, they were affluent and educated, able to travel the world and live a "modern" life. Nicky, for instance, was a talented dancer. She was free to practice her art, including appearing on stages with her head, arms and legs uncovered. Her social life centered around dance and she was making a name for herself as one of the new generation of talented young performers.

Around the same age I was when my mother swept us out of

liberal Christianity into a fundamentalist church, Nicky underwent a very similar upheaval. A changing social and political climate set the scene for a life-changing moment. Nicky remembers the day she and her mother were walking down the street, shopping in one of the more fashionable districts in Tehran. A stranger, garbed from head to toe in the conservative black Muslim "chador," approached them. The woman behind the veil told her mother that she was so beautiful, she could attract harm to herself if she remained uncovered. If she loved her family, she would return to traditional ways. As in the case of my family, mother listened and dad reluctantly followed along, dealing as best he could with the package of restrictions that subsequently descended upon his family.

Tragic consequences For Nicky, this fundamentalist turn had tragic consequences. Forced to don the cumbersome black chador, Nicky was no longer allowed to dance on a stage. In fact, she had to give up all of her favorite physical activities, such as swimming, due to restrictions related to exposing any part of the female body, no matter how innocent the circumstance. Just as my family moved to be closer to the church, Nicky's mother moved the family to a new neighborhood of like-minded Muslims, removing Nicky from public school and sending her to religious school. Most of her classmates were raised from birth in the traditional practices. Nicky struggled with the commandment to pray three times a day and practice Ramadan once a year, including its prescription to fast every day for a month from sunrise to sundown. At prayer meetings held by her mother in their home, Nicky was warned not to do anything to make Allah mad.

This proved to be impossible for the rebellious Nicky. Underneath her chador she wore make-up. She spoke openly to her friends, telling them that she didn't believe in chador because it was not spoken of in the Koran. She protested the rigid rules the girls were being taught, both on the basis of cruelty and inequality. For instance, her teachers insisted that the scriptures dictate that wives must obey their husbands and not question anything they say. Says Nicky: the Koran "does not say women are obligated to serve and cook for men, but the Muslim elders say that a wife must provide everything for him—good love, neat house, and be a good cook." She protested the fact that men got to sit at the front at prayer services, while women were relegated to the back. She deeply resented the fact that if a woman sleeps with a man who is not her husband, she is stoned, and is considered a temptress. The man, however, suffers no punishment. Beneath it all, she rejected the notion being taught to her both at home and at school of a vengeful, punitive patriarchal God. "I believed in a loving God."

Immediately after her graduation from twelfth grade, Nicky removed the chador, stuffed it into a paper bag, and never wore it again. Seeing the political deterioration of Iran, climaxed by the overthrow of the Shah, Nicky was fortunate to get a passport to the United States, where she was able to continue her education. Nicky now has her doctorate, a prestigious appointment at an American university and a job in city government. She and her husband work actively on behalf of women's rights throughout the Islamic world, believing that education and love are the real keys to heaven's gate.

Rebecca: A Jewish Woman's Experience Rebecca was among the older of my conversation partners, a woman in a retirement center who, despite the gray hair and ample wrinkles, retained a lively wit and intellect. Rebecca had been raised in an orthodox Jewish home, loving the warmth of lighting the Sabbath candles and preparing kosher holiday meals with her mother and sisters. While she knew that her father and older brothers held privileged positions within the family, allowed to pass on everyday chores in order to pay attention to their religious studies, Rebecca admired her mother's spunk. Not only did her mother take care of the family, but she held an outside job cooking kosher meals at a Jewish orphanage to keep the family afloat financially.

Like Nicky, as a young girl, Rebecca accepted what outsiders might perceive as inequalities between the sexes as an expression of the man's reverence for the woman. It was "just the way things were" that the men were seated on the main floor of the synagogue while girls and women were allowed only onto the distant balcony. Women never participated in the delivery of the service, reading from the Torah or saying prayers from the bimah—privileges (or as the men would say it, responsibilities)—reserved for men. Nor did they count as one of the ten in a minyan required to hold a service.

Outside influences As a teenager, to help out her family financially, Rebecca took a job in a neighborhood shoe store owned by a family friend. The area, once all Jewish, had been becoming increasingly mixed as young people of many faiths and nationalities who could no longer afford more expensive areas were moving in. In fact, just as her parents were getting serious about finding her a proper orthodox husband from a good family, Rebecca met and fell in love with a conservative Jew. Rebecca can laugh about it now, saying that while she wanted to work, she was certainly not relishing the idea of supporting an orthodox husband's studies while she got stuck as a shop girl the rest of her days. In fact, she wanted to go on to the university and become a librarian. When she finally got up the courage to tell her parents about her plans, they threatened to disown her. Faced with the choice of freedom over tradition, she chose freedom. She and her boyfriend married, raised a family within conservative Judaism, both working in a university setting for many years. Eventually, her parents forgave her and while their relationship was never quite the same, Rebecca never once regretted the decision she made.

Her husband had died several years previously. Rebecca still lights the Sabbath candles, leading the Friday night service at the retirement center. She gets a special kick out of reading Torah to the group, including both men and women who are, incidentally, seated side-by-side.

While the portraits of women raised in the variety of fundamentalist religions in this chapter are drawn with a broad stroke, there are striking similarities of themes and struggles to those of the Protestant fundamentalist women in my formal research. In Part Four of this book, you will meet a number of women raised within Protestant fundamentalism, providing additional depth of understanding the issues faced by women yearning to break free. As with the case of Protestant Christianity, the portraits in this chapter are not meant to be indicative of the experience of women who practice non-fundamentalist forms of these religions, where such versions exist. But for women raised as fundamentalists, the similarities among spiritual and psychological communities of believers are unmistakable and the pain instantly recognizable. We all share a universal hope for a better life and world beyond the confines of toxic fundamentalism.

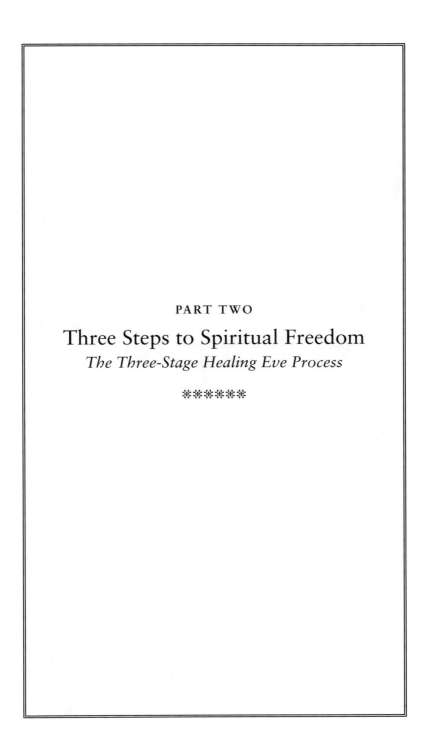

PART TWO

Three Steps to Spiritual Freedom

The Three-Stage Healing Eve Process

CHAPTER FOUR

Stage One: Acknowledging your Programming

I n Part One of *Healing Eve*, I shared with you my own as well as the stories of a number of women who, against the odds, found a way to reclaim their capacity for an authentic life filled with meaning, integrity and joy. At the same time, these stories point to something more: the way to freedom for any woman whose soul cries out from the depths of fundamentalism for a more authentic life. For every one I interviewed, escape from intolerable situations appeared to come about, at least in part, as an unintended by-product of the unplanned twists and turns of fate. In my case, the novelty of television in the 1950s—and its tantalizing window onto the healthy exuberance of adolescent boys and girls dancing on American Bandstand—had somehow managed to escape the all-seeing eyes of the church. For all of us, moves to new communities broke through rigid routines and exposed us to people whose views and beliefs forced us to confront and re-evaluate our lives. For Nicky, Rachel and me, among others, higher education, even when delivered in the context of fundamentalist institutions, inadvertently unearthed parts of ourselves that alternately tantalized and terrified. Somehow, through accidental cracks in the concrete worldview of fundamentalism, we were able to spot glimpses of our authentic selves—sometimes appearing to us as no more than the broken shards of long-buried pottery of an archeologist's dig—but holding the promise of more to come.

PIECING OUR LIVES TOGETHER

For the past several years, I have devoted myself to developing an easy-to-follow process that can guide the woman who yearns for something more, who wants to reclaim her full measure of happiness. The fact that you have found your way to this page is evidence that you have, however haphazardly, already begun your journey to healing your spirit. You don't need me to tell you that there have always been deep stirrings and unrealized potentialities of your authentic self beneath the surface of your life. You may have been in the wrong circumstance to acknowledge or express your authentic voice, but it went underground with you, and now it cries out to you to be retrieved. In this chapter, we take the first step in the process of reclaiming your authentic self. By the end of these next three chapters, you will have the tools to answer your heart's call, reclaiming the options and possibilities the fully-lived life has to offer you.

NORMAL STAGES OF DEVELOPMENT

The social sciences teach us that just as there are normal stages of physical development for human beings, so are there normal stages of psychological, emotional, social and even spiritual development. Many of the women in this book recognize that because of the way they were brought up, they have skipped several important steps in the normal stages of maturation. In particular, the women interviewed for this book frequently described lapses and weaknesses in their development of critical thinking skills and logic. Self-esteem and the development of a healthy ego are also often issues that must be addressed. There's good news, however. As these women's lives illustrate, you can self-select to enter a period of growth in which lost ground can be regained. This doesn't need to be simply a matter of luck or accidental circumstance. You can take specific steps—bring your sincere efforts to the completion of exercises to follow—to arrive at the promised destination. It may not always be easy—but it will always be worthwhile.

CHOOSE THE WAY TO THINK

The first stage of the process that I am going to present to you shortly can help you begin to fill in the missing gaps in your own developmental process, and support your own spirit's efforts to acknowledge and retrieve your authentic self. One of the most important lessons I learned from my work with Dr. Krippner, who co-authored with Dr. Feinstein, *The Mythic Path*, is captured by this quote: "Individuals can choose the way they think...In the process, the emotional residue of experiences that are at the root of self-defeating ways of thinking can also be recognized, healed, and released."

Key to this process in this first stage, *Acknowledgement of Your Programming*, is the recognition, often painful, of what has been missed. In search of the authentic self, we need to dig through the layers upon layers of shaky foundations.

THE WAY IN

Happily, there is an easily identifiable clue as to where to begin looking. Unfortunately, it resides in the exact place that you might well prefer to avoid having to think about: your own self-defeating behaviors.

The process of reflection reminds me of a metaphor shared with me by a friend: "Life is like a big bowl of vegetable soup. If you stop stirring, all the goodies sink to the bottom." My friend who shared her wisdom with me explained that everybody has a favorite vegetable. In my case, it's carrots. And then, there are the vegetables I could do without: onions, for instance. When you put in your spoon, you don't exactly know what you're going to get. And most people, even if they have their preferences, don't sit there and pick out every bit of onion. The flavor comes out of the combination— the integrity of the whole. In other words, you can't get the carrots unless you get a bit of onion from time to time, too. In this spirit, you will shortly be given your first exercises—guided introspection that not only stirs the soup, but gets you sipping hungrily for more. In Dr. Krippner's words: the goal is to target old patterns of belief "that are dysfunctional, even if long held and consistently confirmed by the logic of long-standing beliefs. To the degree you are able to bring about constructive changes in such fundamental perspectives, positive shifts in your life will tend to follow."

THE PROCESS

Before you are guided to identify and begin the process of transformation of your own self-defeating patterns, it will be important for you to confront the nuts and bolts of the worldview to which you were born or introduced at an early age.

The Twenty Question Quiz Access to this information, while deeply buried, is more accessible than you might think. In fact, by taking this twenty question quiz, you will tap into long-buried memories, including the veiled messages that gave you your first sense of what the world was supposed to be about. The purpose of this quiz is to help you identify patterns and influences operative in your life, especially those that were layered over your authentic self when you were a child.

Following are twenty statements to which you merely make note of whether you agree or disagree. You may have a strong reaction to some of these questions. If you do, highlight the statements in question, or better yet, find a journal in which you will want to take notes, and write them down in full. In the next chapter, I will be offering you more suggestions about keeping a journal. At this juncture, you need only consider the possibility of keeping a journal as a private place to record your thoughts. Any notebook will do. But you might find it helpful—as have many of the women in my study—to seek out a special journal, one that beckons especially to you.

While we women who are recovering from fundamentalism share much in common, each of us grew up in circumstances unique to our own individual experience. I'm sure that by the time you answer these first twenty questions, more statements left over from your childhood will have surfaced for you to consider. Go ahead and write them down. Ready?

BY ADOLESCENCE, I KNEW THAT...
(Make note of those with which you strongly agree or disagree.)

		STRONGLY AGREE	AGREE	DISAGREE	STRONGLY DISAGREE
1.	I was perfect just as I was.	○	○	○	○
2.	I was free to discover my own sense of purpose.	○	○	○	○
3.	I was encouraged to look at all the possibilities life had to offer.	○	○	○	○
4.	I could do anything I set my mind to.	○	○	○	○
5.	Even although I was born a female, I felt equal and respected.	○	○	○	○
6.	I was free to explore, entertain any beliefs.	○	○	○	○
7.	I was encouraged to consider all the options and make the best choice for me.	○	○	○	○
8.	I was allowed to question the Bible and church authority.	○	○	○	○
9.	I was allowed to entertain healthy curiosity about sexuality.	○	○	○	○
10.	I was encouraged to have a healthy attitude about my developing body.	○	○	○	○
11.	I was encouraged to take my own needs and desires into consideration before serving the needs of others.	○	○	○	○
12.	I could make mistakes without fear of being sent to hell.	○	○	○	○
13.	I could express my anger in a healthy way.	○	○	○	○
14.	I know I was as good as anybody else.	○	○	○	○
15.	My parents respected me even when my opinions differed from theirs.	○	○	○	○
16.	My authority figures were good role models who walked their talk.	○	○	○	○
17.	What people said is what they did.	○	○	○	○
18.	Mistakes were a natural part of growing up.	○	○	○	○
19.	My opinions mattered: people listened to me.	○	○	○	○
20.	I was cherished and protected by a loving God.	○	○	○	○

Continue writing childhood messages with which you disagree (or agree) in your journal until you have at least a total of 31. In a few minutes, we are going to revisit this list. In the meantime, you can put it aside without having to do anything more about the feelings that have undoubtedly begun surfacing for you. You don't have to know what this "means" about you. You don't have to judge whether you are "right" or "wrong." either. Don't worry about whether you got them all, either. We are simply beginning the process of stirring the soup and seeing what arises. By the end of the process, two chapters from now, you will have been inexorably guided toward the resolution you are seeking. Even without the theory, this process works. So, are you still with me? Good. Why don't we all take a deep breath, and go on to the second step.

SELF-DEFEATING PATTERNS:
PORTAL TO YOUR HIDDEN SELF

In essence, the way into your hidden but authentic self is the portal through which you, as I mentioned earlier, would least like to go: your own self-defeating patterns. There are many self-defeating patterns that can trigger the awareness that there is inner work to be done. Some of the more common indicators are the consistent inability to make a decision, the nagging sense that one is perceived by others differently than how one feels inside, persistent self-neglect of one's physical or emotional needs, free-floating anxiety, shame and so on. At last, we can confront these self-defeating patterns head-on, not as a problem to feel bad about, but as important clues in regard to the retrieval of our hidden selves.

How to get started? Easy. Just answer these simple questions:

1. *What is something I do on a persistent or repetitive basis that no longer serves me?*

In my case, I would write down in my journal: "I have had the tendency all my life to negate my own needs and desires in order to serve the needs of others." After you have a good sense of the self-defeating pattern you will be working with in this exercise (tip: if you take the first one that pops into your mind, you will nine times out of ten have grasped the most fruitful point of entry for you at this time...) go ahead and ask yourself this second key question along with its closely-related follow-up:

2. *Who or what in my life either modeled or encouraged this particular self-destructive pattern of behavior? What, specifically, was the message I received?*

Be as specific as possible, scanning incidents and encounters as early in your life as possible that generated the same negative feelings or behaviors in you or others close to you that you have carried into present time. For inspiration, you may want to revisit the twenty question quiz, looking specifically at those statements with which you had a strong "disagree." Chances are, your memory will be jogged and you will find yourself thinking about family members, church influences and educators who indoctrinated you into worldviews that have long outgrown their usefulness in your life.

In my case, I would write down in my journal: "My mother was the primary example in my life of self-negating physical, intellectual, and emotional needs in order to serve the needs of others first. She reminded me of the Bible scriptures that our religion used to back up a woman's role, based upon the first female in the Bible, Eve." I would then add in some of the Biblical quotations I'd memorized as a child that reinforced this for me.

The tip-off that I tend to self-negate came from my strong "disagree" to question number 11 when taking The Twenty Question Quiz myself: "I was encouraged to take my own needs and desires into consideration before serving the needs of others." The message I received: "Saving other people is more important than taking care of my own emotional needs."

There is one final step to this exercise. Even if you don't believe it to be true, it can be a powerful instigator for reclamation of authenticity in your life. Go ahead and answer this last question:

3. *In regard to the specific self-defeating pattern I am working with, what is the flipside to the primary negative message I received?*

In my case, I would take the message: "Serving the needs of others is more important than taking care of my own needs and desires," and stand it on its head to read: "Serving the needs of others can bring me joy, but not at the expense of taking care of my own needs and desires." It might take some playing around with words to get it right, as there are many possibilities, one of which you will instinctively recognize as being the most direct route to your deepest yearnings: reclamation of your authentic self. After covering several pages with various combinations—even resorting to the dictionary to make sure I had really captured the essence of what I most wanted in my life—I finally settled on the affirmation above. Don't be surprised if you feel some guilt in addition to a sense of elation you may feel when you uncover the essence of your authentic healing affirmation. For many of us, even to admit what it is we really want for ourselves—what we deserve—let alone submit the words to paper—runs counter to a lifetime of negative programming. Again, you don't have to believe this positive affirmation to be true for yourself at this stage. In fact, how you are feeling is absolutely right for you—the fastest route to retrieval of your authentic self. Of course, at this or any stage of this process, should you feel overwhelmed with emotion—sensing sadness, doubts or any other emotion that you do not feel equipped to handle by yourself—please seek professional guidance. Many of us have needed the help of a compassionate friend, therapist or advisor to hold our hand through the process of retrieval. I mean, sometimes we pull up the spoon and there is a bit of onion. Sometimes, we pull up the spoon and there is nothing but *onions*. Giving yourself the gift of qualified assistance when you need it is also a sign of recovery. By the way, obviously you received more than one negative message in your life. And, unfortunately, you most probably have more than one self-defeating pattern as well. So I encourage you to repeat this process as often as you like, flipping as many self-defeating patterns as you think might be helpful to you. If you are like me, you will want to make sure that the journal you select has many, many pages! When you have captured the essence of your childhood programming, you are ready to progress to the next stage in the Healing Eve Process: Healing your Reactivity.

CHAPTER FIVE

Stage Two: Healing your Reactivity

F eeling some sense of trepidation, confusion or anxiety is not a problem with the process, however. In fact, during this second stage, feeling any of a thousand negative emotions on the spectrum from sadness to despair is perfectly normal. I'm sure it feels anything but normal to you. Perhaps one of the reasons you are feeling so disoriented is you have entered into the transitional stage of growth in the life cycle that, according to developmental psychologists, is commonly associated with adolescence. Chances are that your adolescent years are behind you—and yet, here you are feeling the pain of new, growing awareness that seems somehow not to fit your concept of who you thought you were and how the world worked. At the same time, your tender awareness of your more authentic dreams, yearnings, feelings and wishes are still far too vulnerable to be truly put to the test. You wonder if the possibilities you've glimpsed will ever grow strong enough to really make their way into the world. And even more frightening, if they do, what changes will you have to make in your life—and will the new future you envision really be better than the security of the familiar you are working so hard to shed?

Try not to judge yourself for having to stop now to go back and pick up the missing pieces. As the psychologists consistently inform us, healthy psycho-spiritual growth depends on a period of disorder out of which the reconstituted authentic self shall emerge. In this critical stage of your journey, you will learn how to experience the pain of transition not as a problem to be solved—but as an indication that you have seriously begun a period of promising and fruitful personal growth .

DISILLUSIONMENT

What makes this stage of the process so emotionally challenging? The answer can be summarized in one word: Disillusionment. Again, we tend to think of disillusionment as a bad or negative thing. While the experience of disillusionment is painful, that doesn't make it bad. Think about it. When we become disillusioned, we are, in truth, becoming aware of old beliefs, messages and behaviors that were based on illusion. We realized that those things that we were taught—the ideals to which we were meant to aspire—are not in sync with our innermost knowing. We are literally "Dis-illusioned."

Unfortunately, we do not just snap our fingers and replace one set of beliefs with another. Even if we sense intellectually and emotionally what a healthier belief might be, there is going to be a period of conflict and mourning over the loss of original direction and sense of purpose. Not only can you anticipate conflict with others who do not want you to change, you may be feeling inner conflict, as well. The conflict increases the more you open yourself to new information, influences and depths of self-knowledge. In fact, disillusionment serves as the growth edge of your emotional development, admitting to yourself that even those myths that once offered effective guidance must be relinquished—even if you have no idea of what's to come. If you continue to hang on to the past, you will repeatedly find yourself in situations that damage you. You will feel restricted and burdened. Through the healthy process of disillusionment, the old views of the world and self are acknowledged as being outdated or dysfunctional, allowing you to glimpse and nurture more authentic, healthier views of the world and self.

Traditionally, the social sciences refer to this period between worldviews as "liminal." Anthropologists study initiatory rites of passage, rituals common to many pre-modern cultures. In the classic initiation, the adolescent child is separated from the familiarity of everyday life of his or her tribe and is put through a series of torturous tests. Transformed by the experience, the initiate re-enters the tribe at ritual's end as an adult, with a new role and persona. William Bridges, in his book *Transitions*, relates the anthropological studies to modern psychology with respect to individuals in transition at any stage of their lives. Paraphrasing Bridges, the period of disorientation is marked by a sense of "lostness" and emptiness, before life resumes an intelligible pattern and direction. Individuals going through this stage describe their experience as feeling "stuck, dead, lost in some great, dark non-world." As unpleasant as they are, the negative emotional states are natural and inevitable, comprising a kind of symbolic death for the "person-that-she-had-been." According to Bridges, the ending process centers around four Ds: disengagement, disidentification, disenchantments and disorientation.

Disengagement has to do with the emotional and spiritual separation from the contexts within which we have come to know ourselves. For many of the women I interviewed, disengagement was initiated by—and in some cases precipitated—a physical relocation. Other factors influence us to disengage, however. Divorce, career or job transitions, death of family members, serious illness and many other definitive events disengage us from our familiar place in the social order.

Disidentification is closely related to disengagement—the natural result of becoming dislocated from the familiar routines of our lives. Removed from the status quo, we experience the loss of the role we have been playing for many years: a role that prescribed our behavior. There is no shorthand for how we see ourselves: whether it be daughter, wife, good girl, religious person or whatever mental picture we had of ourselves. In its place, are discomfort and an endless parade of questions and confusions. The sense of loneliness can be unbearable, as one realizes that the very people, environment and resources that one is having doubts about are the very places one used to turn to for advice and comfort.

Disenchantment is closely related to the loss of familiar routines, locations and roles. It is the recognition that what one always thought of as being "reality" is no longer to be trusted. In the words of Bridges, "The lesson of disenchantment is the discovery that in order to change, you must realize that some significant part of your old reality was in your head, not out there." Bridges points out that in this stage, almost inevitably, there is the sense that one has been cheated—as though someone or something tricked us. "At such times, we need to consider whether the old view or belief may not have been an enchantment cast on us in the past to keep us from seeing deeper into ourselves and others than we were then ready to. The disenchantment experience is the signal that the time has come to look below the surface of what has been thought to be so."

Looking below the surface brings us the final D: disorientation. Disorientation occurs in the void between what was and what will be. As we peel away the protective layers that have turned toxic on us, we expose to the light of day not only the possibilities of what may be, contained within the shards of our authenticity— but the unearthing of old memories of shame and hurt, as well. Even if we are into our fifties or sixties when we arrive at this stage, we experience the sadness of the abused child, the turmoil of the rebellious teenager and the confusion of the misplaced adult—all at once.

THE FASTEST WAY THROUGH

Confrontation with the exposed self may seem hopeless to the woman traversing this portion of the journey, but the truth is that it is the source of all hope. The key is that at exactly the same moment the recovering Christian fundamentalist is doubting her conception of God and the divine, she must make her greatest leap of faith. In the words of Bridges: "One must surrender and give into the emptiness and stop struggling to escape it. Chaos is not a mess, but rather it is the primal state of pure energy to which the person returns for every true new beginning. It is only from the perspective of the old form that chaos looks fearful—from any other perspective, it looks like life itself, as yet unshaped by purpose and identification."

One of the ways to give up resistance is to make the conscious effort to turn towards, rather than away from, the pain. We began doing this in the first stage of the process, shared with you in the previous chapter, when I asked you to identify self-defeating patterns in your current life. By doing so, you would gain the most direct access to those old messages, self-images, outlived dreams and beliefs that have become toxic to you. Just as the archeologist must first clean the shards before they can be reassembled, so is it vital for you to tend to your emotional and spiritual wounds. Inevitably, you will be forced to surface old memories you wish you could somehow avoid confronting. However, recall that childhood issues leftover from previous stages must be handled or they will undermine subsequent stages of development. This is especially challenging for children raised within fundamentalism, who were trained from an early age to avoid questioning the precepts of their faith. My own life story and the women who participated in my research gave me the clues to the differences between normal development and development in the fundamentalist child. Even though it may be more difficult for us, it is not too late to begin filling in the missing pieces.

HEALING THE REACTIVE SELF

For each of the women in my study, there was a haphazard quality to the initiation of the stage I refer to as "Healing the Reactive Self." All of us accidentally found ourselves in situations where we were exposed to competing points of view, many of which held the promise of a peace and integrity we had not even known was possible. Chances are that you, too, are already involved in the awakening process. You may not even know how or why your old status quo began to pinch and squeeze, like a pair of shoes meant for somebody else's feet. But the fact that you are still reading is evidence that your journey has begun in earnest. Rather than continue to depend on luck, you are now in the position to become even more proactive in the reclamation of spiritual freedom. While you wish this were quick, easy work, understand that in order to retrieve a life of integrity and joy for yourself, you must first discipline yourself to dig toward rather than away from the pain. Shall we continue?

PRACTICES

Confronting your pain does not mean allowing yourself to be victimized by your past. Surrendering to the pain of your transition, ironically, takes work and discipline. The following exercises have been designed to create the optimum environment in which your deepest healing can transpire.

In the last chapter, I suggested that you begin a journal— promising to say more about this invaluable support for personal growth. The reason I am such a strong advocate of journaling is that so many of my participants told me that writing in a daily journal was their primary vehicle toward healing. Even if it felt like a chore at the time, they could revisit their entries months or years later, recognizing how much they had grown.

Approaching journaling as a chore is common among women breaking free from fundamentalism, as the process asks you to uncover emotions, thoughts and desires that are not to be entertained by fundamentalism. But being willing to make the attempt to put your experiences into words—as challenging as it will be—contains the key to retrieving your authentic self. Important parts of ourselves that we have silenced, hidden, or previously refused to admit to, will surface. Thinking and feeling about your life in a disciplined way will help you put the pieces of your life back together.

So what is the discipline of journaling? It is, in fact, not only the conduit to admitting to your pain—it is also the antidote. As I wrote in the last chapter, you can make journaling a productive experience by selecting a special journal that holds the promise of better things to come for you. It will also be important to find a pleasant, private environment in which to write daily. Set aside a period of time in which you are unlikely to be disturbed: a half-hour to an hour should be more than adequate to get you started. Eventually, you will find the time and rhythm that best suits your needs and desires.

What should you write about? After awhile, you may find yourself overflowing with words you can't wait to commit to paper: not dissimilar to the anticipation of talking things over with an old, dear friend. But for women raised in fundamentalism, more structured assignments may be in order for quite some time. This is true for those of us who have difficulty remembering our childhood pain—and equally true for those of us who already mull too much over the unhappy aspects of our lives. In order to reap the benefits of introspection, it is vital that you keep in mind that the reason you are journaling is to do the hard work of retrieving the broken shards of your authentic self, mending them back together to be whole again. These assignment suggestions are designed to keep you on track.

SPECIFIC JOURNAL SUGGESTIONS

Revisit Your Childhood Messages In the previous chapter, you took The Twenty Question Quiz, twenty statements leading you to insight about messages you received—or from which you were deprived—that have proven to be toxic to your mental, emotional and spiritual health. Before you begin, get out your journal and turn to a fresh page. Write today's date at the top before reading your previous entries. In particular, take a look at your responses to the "Twenty Question Quiz" and begin with the statements to which you had the strongest response: positive or negative. Each day, take one of these statements and let it bring up memories, feelings and thoughts from your past. The emotions may be happy or sad, angry or upset. For example, if you had a strong negative response to the question "My opinions mattered: people listened to me," copy this question onto the page just below today's date and begin asking yourself probing questions. Don't worry about whether your answers are grammatically correct, or even coherent. The most important part of this process is to let your authentic feelings flow out of your heart, through your pen and onto the page.

In response to this sample message, one logical place to begin would be to recall a time in your life when you had something important to say and your opinion was ignored, brushed aside or even met with anger or resistance. Recreate as much of this memory as possible, asking yourself such questions as: *How did you feel? Did you feel sorry for yourself? Did you feel lonely? Punished? Afraid?*

Let one thought flow into another. *How were you punished in your family? Were you frozen out? Or did you walk on egg shells, knowing that physical or emotional abuse might be heaped upon you for the slightest infraction?*

Now you can dig deeper. *Was there a time when you withheld your true opinion, knowing that you would not be heard, anyway? How important was it to you that you win or maintain your parents' and community's approval?*

Now go deeper still: *What do you think was going on in the minds and hearts of your parents or other people important to you when they refused to take your opinions seriously? How did their attitudes and beliefs about life influence their response to you?*

And now, as deep as you can go: *In what ways do you still squash your true opinions in order to win or maintain approval from the people around you? In what kinds of situations do you feel valued and heard? In what situations do you fall back into childhood patterns of approval and self-protection? Can you think of a time recently that bears some similarity to your childhood pattern? How about today?*

Every day, revisit and write about one of the statements from the quiz that you feel strongly about. You can write about a particularly toxic message over and over again, continuing to retrieve memories, thoughts and feelings and exposing them to the light of day. Or you can go on to any one of the other twenty plus questions. (The ideal is to come up with at least 31, one for each day of the month.) Try to do this every day, even if you don't get an immediate sense of relief or breakthrough. In fact, it is important not to put any pressure on yourself or this process. Rather, be content to commit only to being truthful with yourself. Over time, you will begin to realize that you are thinking more clearly about your past and present issues. You will come to understand that your current problems did not come to you out of the blue, but rather developed over a long period of time as organic, if toxic, parts of the emotional atmosphere within which you were raised. Without having to do anything more about this than self-reflect as honestly as you can, you will find yourself starting to heal.

Make a Wish List   While healing your reactive self is natural and organic, it is not simple. For even while you mourn the loss of the familiarity of your childhood beliefs—even those that have been harmful to you—you are also asked to be open to signs of recovery. One of the first signs of hope is your ability to day-dream about the possibilities. Now would be a good time to take out your journal and make a wish list for yourself. Ask yourself this question: *If I were free to express my soul fully—what would my life look like one year from now?* Imagine yourself in particular circumstances and see what you are doing. *Who are you relating to? What is it that you really want for yourself? How's your health? How's your spirit?*

Once you have a strong sense of what it is you want for yourself, close your eyes and visualize it with as much detail as possible. Many spiritual masters, philosophies and religions teach visualization techniques, by which you imagine the future you want for yourself in as striking and complete detail as possible, providing the opportunity for your dreams to become manifest in the world. Medical doctor, Christiane Northrup, M.D., author of *Women's Bodies, Women's Wisdom: Creating Physical and Emotional Health and Healing*, is not what you'd traditionally call a "mystic." However, she believes that if you focus on a thought or feeling without introducing a contradicting thought or emotion for just 17 seconds, "you'll see evidence of this thought manifest around you in the physical world."

If 17 seconds could be so powerful, how about an hour? Put on some inspiring music, get yourself into a comfortable position, and actively imagine yourself (mentally or in your journal) in a particular scene and moment in which you are having the kind of spiritually free life you'd like. What are you doing? Where are you? What are you thinking? Imagine the smells, the sounds, the temperature of the air on your skin. What are you wearing? What's the expression on your face? Are other people in the vicinity? What is their reaction to you? Just how joyful do you feel? Now imagine yourself doubling the joy! When the joy has permeated every cell of your body, go ahead and open your eyes. As you do, make sure to keep the feelings of joy with you as you return to your day's routines.

In the next chapter, you will come to understand more fully how all of the hard work you've been doing can begin paying off in earnest, as you emerge from the transitional stage of disillusionment and enter into the third and final stage: Reclaiming your Wisdom.

CHAPTER SIX

Stage Three: Reclaiming your Wisdom

I n the beginning, I promised you a happy ending. That happy ending is now upon us. By the end of this chapter, you will have completed the three-stage Healing Eve Process, utilizing all the tools you need to reclaim a life of integrity, joy and meaning for yourself. By now, however, you may well be suspecting that for women raised in fundamentalism, there is more to "happiness" than first meets the eye. In the case of happiness, the "more" places the experience of authenticity above all else. So before we continue, let's revisit how I came to my definition of what it means to be authentic.

THE ACTUALIZED SELF

During my doctoral studies, you will recall that I encountered the thinking of developmental psychologists. Essentially, the work of these theorists centers around the same core concept. Whether they place the emphasis on physical, spiritual, mental or emotional components, each contends that there is a normal cognitive/psychological sequence of stages through which the healthy individual progresses. In every one of these models, there is some culmination representing, in the words of Abraham Maslow, the actualized self: the realization of one's full potential as a human being. It is this stage of development that that we refer to as Healing Eve.

Recently, a friend gifted me with a copy of self-help author Wayne Dyer's *10 Secrets for Success and Inner Peace*. One chapter title particularly caught my eye: "Don't Die With Your Music Still In You." For some reason, I thought back to one of the last interviews I had with one of my research participants, Carmen, a woman you will meet "formally" in part four. In particular, I recalled an image of Carmen's baby, Kirk, sleeping peacefully in her arms while Carmen told a story about her Great Grandma. Great Grandma had taken the young Carmen to a Pentecostal revival, terrifying the child by screaming nonsense syllables while banging her fist repeatedly on the chair before her. Fearing her Great Grandma had been possessed by demons, the young Carmen ran to strangers in a nearby pew, hoping to find safety. As you will come to know, Carmen walked a long hard road to finally find safe harbor in her life—and to provide it for her son. In place of the garbled tongues that had terrified her as a child, Carmen had learned to voice a new kind of prayer.

"I don't pray for forgiveness and I don't pray out of fear," Carmen had shared with me earlier that day. "Instead, I feel and express gratitude. I pray because I'm thankful for what I have…I honestly believe if I died tonight I would not be scared about what would happen to my soul. I now choose to act as if this is it: we only have one chance. This is my one opportunity to do what I have to do."

WHAT'S YOUR MUSIC?

In her profound love for her son—and her dedication to protecting him from the terrors that had shadowed her own childhood—Carmen had found the way to express the music in her. "Don't Die With Your Music Still in You," the open page on my lap cried out to me. What was the music in me that yearned to express itself? Of course, it was the passion I was feeling at that very moment: pursuing my dream of a doctorate in a field that would help me unravel the riddle of my fundamentalist childhood. My passion had led me to invest the time, effort and energy to track down others who had defied the odds, who had healed Eve and refused to deny their unsung song. At that moment, I knew that I would not only get my doctorate—but that I would turn my dissertation on the subject into the very book you are reading today. This, then, is my song—the music long denied—that despite everything, I would not let die.

The potential to actualize one's self from the beginning is hypothesized by many of the developmental theorists I studied. Fulfillment of this potential, however, is not a free and easy ascent. And as addressed in the previous chapter, for female fundamentalists, in particular, the normal stages of development are routinely delayed, halted or skipped entirely. Over and over again, we are asked to deny our own sense of right and wrong, our own opinions, feelings and innate ability to think for ourselves, and to adopt—without question—the fundamentalist worldview. Our real selves are buried beneath other people's and institution's agendas. Recognition of this is the core task of the first stage of Healing Eve. This is when we surface and address our original programming. We are taught that if we disagree with what the authorities are teaching us, it is we who are crazy, bad or doomed. The belief that even as a woman, you have a mind worth nurturing, or a genuine affinity for people of other faiths and races, or the belief that, as an adolescent, having a developing body is a healthy, natural thing could be undermined by the old messages about Eve's sin in the Garden of Eden. In the case of Christian fundamentalism, we are condemned to an eternity in hell. Is it any wonder that our original, authentic impulses, responses, ideals and potentials failed to thrive? Earlier in the chapter, we discussed William Bridge's four Ds: disengagement, disidentification, disenchantment and disorientation. These, along with my own favorite D word, disillusionment, comprise the primary means of confronting head on the painful lapses in our cognitive, psychological, emotional and spiritual growth.

Confronting disillusion constitutes the second stage of the Healing Eve Process, in which we face and heal our reactivity. During this transitional stage, we struggle with the realization that the world of our parents—and even more disturbing, much of what has been taught to us about God, Himself—is made-up. And made-up, not only as some innocent fairy story meant to comfort or educate—but to control and manipulate us. At the moment of our awakening, we confront the losses all at once—and we are horrified. Yet out of the abyss comes new conviction. The women I studied for this book became inspired to reclaim their lives, no matter the cost. While actualizing one's full potential for a meaningful life is not an easy or pain free task for any women in our society, for those of us who struggle to come into our own out of the depths of fundamentalism, the challenge is even more daunting. It is our lot to engage in a disciplined and committed effort, making up lost stages and reclaiming our original potential to be authentically, fully human.

THE DEFINITION OF AUTHENTIC

At last, we approach the nuts and bolts of the final stage of the process, in which we reclaim our wisdom. Each of the women in my study, all of whom are actively engaged in the reclamation of their wisdom, expressed in her own special way the profound joy and satisfaction that comes from the realigning of soul with reality. We may speak of it as happiness, but the experience of wisdom born of authenticity is far more complex—and the pay-off far richer. Of course, we want to feel good, to have fun and experience ourselves as secure and loved. Many of us, having literally gone through hell to reclaim a worldview that offers the possibility of attaining our own rather than somebody else's dream, are more likely to reach these exalted states on a more consistent basis. When we do, we have no doubts that the hard work has paid off and that we are, indeed, fulfilling our human potential. But what catches us by surprise is that even when we are in pain—at those difficult times when we find ourselves struggling with doubts, anger, sadness or any other of the darker tones on the emotional scale—we still think the path we've chosen away from fundamentalism and toward our authentic lives is a journey well worth taking. Enjoying spiritual freedom, we can embrace our physical, mental and emotional states as healthy, logical responses to the real issues we face in our lives—here and now. We don't need to be perfect, to sacrifice ourselves as martyrs, to see things in black and white or to judge ourselves against external standards in order to embrace ourselves as worthy of trust, reliance and belief. Having declared authorship of our own lives, we revel in the profoundly hard-won fact that we are, indeed, authentic.

SYNTHESIS, NOT REJECTION

In the first flush of freedom, it is tempting to want to leave the past definitively behind. In the previous stages, recognizing the damage inflicted upon us by the fundamentalist world view, it is natural that we would react bitterly to what turned out in many respects to be a bill of goods. For some time now, we have allowed ourselves to feel the full brunt of the pain of our disappointment. We have given vent to our anger and our disillusionment. We have made the attempt to turn our backs on our pasts and try on different realities, often as divorced from our upbringing as we can muster. There is support for this definitive rejection of the past in the popular culture. Many self-help books argue that we should make the effort to expunge our pasts in order to live fully in the present moment. Given the broad and deep pain of our fundamentalist roots, annihilating the past is a concept that holds much appeal. However, my research shows an alternate route to the present moment, more suited to the needs of recovering fundamentalists whose pasts are not so easily dismissed. This is the path that I took and the path that I have come to recognize as inherent in the recovery of every one of the women in my study who are reaping the benefits of the authentic life.

I would propose that in this third and final phase of the Healing Eve Process, the essential task is not to ignore or forget our pasts, but rather, to make peace with our personal histories. This does not mean that we surrender any of our human potential out of misplaced loyalty, guilt or fear. But rather, that we use everything we've got—including our pasts—to fuel our personal growth. We do this through a process that personal mythologists refer to as "synthesis." Stage three of the Healing Eve Process, "Reclaiming your Wisdom," is the phase in which this synthesis occurs. At last, we move beyond the victimization of the first stage and the rebellion and reactivity of the second. In this culminating phase, opposing tensions become assimilated and a new, guiding message emerges. The hallmark of the authentic life that arises is integrity: an embrace of all our selves—programmed and reactive—the sum of which constitutes a whole greater than any of the parts. It is this wholeness that can be summed up in one word: authenticity. Authenticity is real and unshakable specifically because it does not leave anything out, even as it transcends everything that has come before to be fresh and appropriate in the present moment.

In this, the third stage of the healing process, we have the opportunity to complete the unfinished work of childhood and adolescence—regardless of whatever age we happen to be—and establish a mature relationship not only with our parents, but to the worldview with which they came bundled.

If we can learn to forgive our parents, we can begin to see more clearly the good as well as the bad in the residue of our childhoods.

You may have hated the minister's harping on eternal damnation, but you may have cherished your memories of the choir's harmonious singing about sweet Jesus' love. You may have resented the rote memorization of scripture but loved the act of silent prayer. Even if you disliked every bit of the content and rigidity, surely you recognize value in the general idea of providing children with some sense of structure. Perhaps you loved the parables but hated the community, or loved the community but disliked how they treated outsiders. Is there nothing at all to be salvaged?

Not long after I forgave my parents, while embarking upon my doctoral research, I had a telling dream. In this dream, I was standing before a bureau of drawers. One by one, I pulled out objects from the drawers, examining each one to see if it were still good. I pulled out a shoe, an old stuffed bear, a book. I don't remember the exact nature of each item, but the meaning was clear. I was to revisit my childhood influences, beliefs and messages and determine which were to be discarded—and which were still valid. This was the beginning of the intellectual and spiritual journey that culminated in my spiritual freedom.

CONCLUSION

Having come this far is no small accomplishment. You have found the way to fulfilling your true human potential, answering the cries of your spirit echoing from the depths in search of a more authentic life. It is your desire to live wisely that will deliver to you the resolution you seek. Already, you are one of the courageous women who, against the odds, has found a way to reclaim your capacity for a life filled with meaning, integrity and joy. You have become willing to do whatever it takes to reclaim your soul. You are already something even better than being happy. You are Healing Eve.

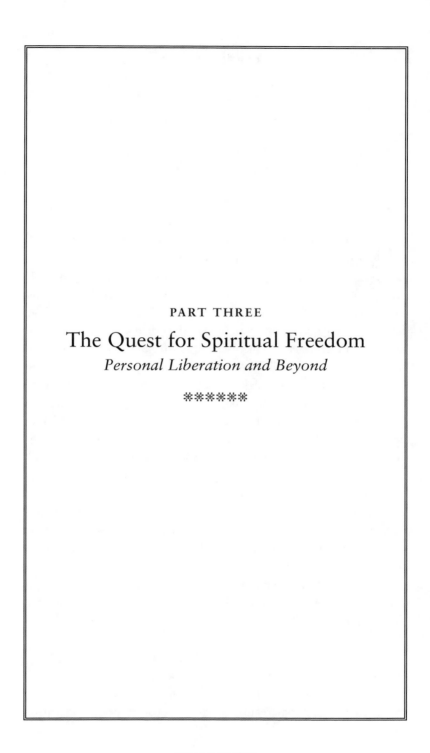

PART THREE

The Quest for Spiritual Freedom
Personal Liberation and Beyond

❋❋❋❋❋❋

CHAPTER SEVEN

Dogma-Free Spirituality

Behold, these things that I do,
you can do even greater.
JESUS

After leaving the toxicity of fundamentalism behind, what is the best one can hope for in terms of the reclamation of some kind of spiritual life? The answer is: a great deal. In fact, my research reveals that most women who leave fundamentalism do not, as one might expect, turn away from religion completely. Rather than describe themselves as religious, however, most refer to themselves as spiritual. Very often, the women incorporate belief in a spiritual realm and/or transcendent being into their new worldview. While shunning anything that even hints at religious dogma, they express a surprising degree of nostalgia concerning certain favorite aspects of their religious upbringing, be it the Lord's Prayer, the Passover Seder or The Golden Rule. With the maturity and release that comes with authenticity, they recognize the love, faith and hope that were masked by strict interpretations of religious beliefs by which they were raised. When stripped of punitive overtones, most are capable now of recognizing the life-affirming potential of these beliefs. No longer confined by institutional walls and intercessors, many of my co-researchers reported an experience of power greater than themselves while climbing to the top of a mountain, getting their hands in the dirt while gardening, listening to a piece of classical music, and the like.

WHAT IS SPIRITUALITY?

When I speak of spirituality, I use the term in a very broad sense to refer to beliefs that describe the potential to transcend ordinary existence and material reality. Spiritual devotion does not depend upon membership in any specific institution, attendance at events or gatherings or an authority figure to intercede and interpret for God. Needless to say, spirituality was not what you'd call a "buzzword" in the community within which I was raised. Even now, it is almost too good to be true that religion and spirituality can be linked.

Previously, I gave a definition for the word soul that is helpful here: Soul: "The animating and vital principle in human beings, credited with the faculties of thought, action, and emotion and often conceived as an immaterial entity...the vital core." (American Heritage College Dictionary, 3rd Ed.) It is spirituality that accesses and gives expression to soul. As the definition implies, the experience of spirituality is akin to authenticity—but it is something more. It is, in fact, mind and spirit working together towards the common goal of integrity: wholeness experienced as holiness.

MASLOW'S UNDERSTANDING

Psychologist Abraham Maslow, whom I have cited previously, describes these direct experiences of that something more as "peak experiences." Arguing against the notion that only ordained officials can receive direct revelations from God, Maslow's research concluded, "From the viewpoint of the peak experience each person has his own private religion, which he develops out of his own private revelations in which are revealed to his own private myths and symbols, rituals, and ceremonials... These transcendent experiences seem to occur more frequently in people who have rejected their inherited religion and have then created one for themselves." Maslow reached this conclusion by studying mature, psychologically healthy individuals, confidently asserting that there is a presence within human beings of a tendency toward self-actualization, a state that encompasses compassion, creativity, ethics, love and spirituality.

FIRST ENCOUNTER

My first encounter with spirituality came outside of my church experience, on forbidden territory and terms that my mother would have been quick to label "heathenism." My first memory of the word "spiritual" came when I was 25, having left home to live in

California. In Texas, when you greet somebody, just about the first question out of your mouth is "What church do you belong to?" It's a shorthand way to situate people, what in other regions would be expressed as "So, what do you do for a living?" or even "What's your sign?" So, when I posed the question "What religion are you?" to a new acquaintance, you can imagine my surprise when she answered: "No religion in particular. I'm spiritual." I had never heard of such a thing—but I knew instantly that I wanted something of what she had. It was my first taste of spiritual freedom, the revolutionary notion that one could be free to explore the cornucopia of spiritual options available to the authentic self. My convictions were confirmed when soon after, I bumped into a woman my age I'd met at women's group at the church I had joined. "I haven't seen you in ages," I said over groceries. "Why don't you come to group any more?" She threw her beautiful blond hair back and laughed. "I operate differently. When the spirit leads me to stay home with the kids, I follow the spirit. Lately, spirit's been telling me that Wednesday mornings is time to do the ironing—and I don't feel guilty at all."

The notion of hearing directly from God without an interpreter in the middle swept through me. I determined to give it a try. I decided to seek out a beautiful, quiet place in nature and simply listen. Would spirit speak to me? Perhaps it wasn't such a foreign notion, after all. On one of my early forays—to a rose garden tucked in the corner of a city park—I suddenly remembered a favorite mountain cabin, which my family regularly visited, even after our baptisms. The church authorities looked askance at anything that could compete with our attendance at the various church services and activities that filled our schedules week after week. But my father had stood up to community pressure to take all of us to the mountains instead of church from time to time. I realized suddenly that the mountains were where my father went to get nurtured. Father, too, loved to garden and one of my favorite childhood memories is the gardenia plant that he had planted right beneath my bedroom window. Perhaps the fruit doesn't fall that far from the tree, after all. It may be no surprise, for instance, that one of the reasons I am attracted to archeology is that it gives me the opportunity to go to out of the way places in nature, getting my own hands into the dirt. While I have now seen many of the oldest and rarest treasures ever retrieved from the earth, one of the most meaningful finds I ever personally witnessed was a simple abalone shell embedded with a small crystal unearthed at a Gabrielino Indian burial site on San Clemente Island. The shell told the story of a woman whose life had been determined by the cycles of planting, harvesting, fishing and cooking. The crystal, taken from the earth, bespoke a love of beauty and a sense of the eternal. Those who had once lost a woman special to them had left it for us to find centuries later—this simple but eloquent token of their love. I was astonished to discover that God could, indeed, speak to me without an interpreter. I now go as often as I can to places quiet enough to hear over the hubbub of our daily lives, which so often distracts us from what really matters. Recently, I took my grandson to Sedona, Arizona, hiking amongst the silent Red Rocks. It happened to be a Sunday morning. We climbed up dirt and gravel paths onto the gently rounded rocks. At the top, we sat and took in the magnificent view. "It's almost like God is here," Robert whispered. "He is," I whispered back.

"Formal" spirituality came to me in a way that I was not expecting years after I began simply to wander and listen. For years, I'd been paying an annual visit to a local health spa, enjoying the solitude, as well as social time with other women. One year I arrived and there was a new offering side-by-side with yoga and massage. A meditation instructor was on hand, introducing me to the world of disciplined meditation and journaling. I'll never forget the first time the instructor told the class "The answers are inside us." I thought again of my mother's fervent warnings against heathenism, and steeled myself against her predictable response when I called from the spa to tell her what I was up to. Mother was, indeed, shocked, but she was three states away. I thought but did not communicate the intoxicating sense of freedom that swept over me. *"What are you going to do? Send me to my room?"*

WHAT SPIRITUALITY IS NOT

The notion of having the answers inside of us—especially for women—runs counter to fundamentalist belief. Women, in particular, are meant to be kept "in line" by the church. As you recall, in the words of Timothy:

> *Let the woman learn in silence with all subjection.*
> *But I suffer not a woman to teach or to usurp authority*
> *over the man, but to be in silence. For Adam was first formed*
> *and then Eve, and Adam was not deceived, but the woman*
> *being deceived was in the transgression.*
>
> I TIMOTHY (2:11–14)

It is, as expressed to me by one of my research participants, "One of the most cruel things that one can do to another, and this is to quiet your voice". Teresa, a Native American whom you met briefly in the introduction and will get to know better in section four, had just shared with me the richness of her own original beliefs, taught to her by Grandmother Corn. There was The Breath, harmony with nature, respect for the feminine—all rudely interrupted by the entrance of the missionaries. To this day, my own eyes well up with tears as I remember what Teresa said next. "Here we have all of these female supernaturals who lived with us in such a feminine world. Then here suddenly are these church people who come to be in our lives, bringing with them this male deity. I really, really do resent that in the Christian belief system—it's the male that becomes a supernatural, and I wonder, 'How come that happened?'" A lot of women—scholars included—having been asking this question, allowing both their passion and their intellectual curiosity to guide their theories and research. Foremost are the feminist academics in history, archeology, sociology, anthropology and religious studies. In the seminal feminist text, *The Second Sex*, French scholar Simone DeBeauvoir writes:

> "Man enjoys the great advantage of having a god
> endorse the code he writes; and since man exercises a
> sovereign authority over women it is especially

fortunate that this authority has been vested in him by the Supreme Being."

"For the Jews, Mohammedans and Christians among others, man is master by divine right. The fear of God will therefore repress any impulse towards revolt in the downtrodden female."

A WAY OUT

Earlier, I mentioned one of the attractions to me of archeology: being able to legitimately dig in the dirt of mother earth to your heart's content. Perhaps there is a second reason: my need to definitively, consciously see for myself that the material reality of the Garden of Eden myth was being called into question by people I respected in the scientific community. From the time I was old enough to understand such things, the Christian fundamentalist instructors were pleased to share with me the exact year Eve convinced Adam to eat of the fruit: That would have been 4004 B.C.: the "known" date of the beginning of humankind. They knew this definitively because the date had been worked out by Archbishop Usher in 1650 A.D. Using my rational capabilities, given to me by God, I became convinced otherwise—that based upon geological and paleoanthropological data, the earth is actually between four and five billion years old. Having personally held in my hands hominid fossil remains from Olduvai Gorge, Tanzania, dated at 2–1/2 million years old, I felt a surge of certainty that the date of the Garden of Eden creation story must be called into question. Even more liberating, the theology, too, was crumbling beneath my trembling fingers. In its place, spiritual freedom was being birthed.

I now stand both intellectually and spiritually with individuals who are both scientists and believers in a higher power: people like Episcopal bishop John Shelby Spong, who wrote in *Rescuing the Bible from Fundamentalism* that it is not only our right, but our duty to update our religion based upon scientific discoveries made through the years.

"The Bible relates to us the way our ancient forebears understood and interpreted their world, made sense out of life, and thought about God. Our task is the same as theirs. We must interpret our world in the light of our knowledge and suppositions...The Bible becomes not a literal road map to reality but a historic narrative of the journey our religious forebears made in the eternal human quest to understand life, the world, themselves, and God."

SPIRITUALITY AS PARTNERSHIP

Feminist scholars and liberal theologians have carried the load in terms of updating the narratives that help us envision a world in which, no longer dominated by male stereotypes, women and men are in partnership with each other—and with God. This entails no less than a rebalancing of our view of life with the feminine, from a male God who has all the power to the revolutionary notion of all of us, including women, as co-creators. This is not just wishful thinking. In the *Chalice and the Blade*, Scholar Riane Eisler talks of evidence of an ancient culture where women and men lived in harmony with each other and with nature. Eisler suggests, through an examination of the archeological evidence, that the "war of the sexes" is neither divine nor biologically determined. "It provides verification that a better future is possible—and is in fact firmly rooted in the haunting drama of what actually happened in the past." While a full report is beyond our current scope, Eisler cites findings that indicate the existence of a society, circa 5700 to 5000 B.C.E. located on the Anatolian plain, that was equalitarian with no marked distinctions based on either class or sex. There is no evidence of weaponry, but the chalice—a symbol for the divine feminine—was much revered. The interruption of what Eisler calls this "partnership model" occurred when a male-dominated culture from the north swarmed down on the peaceful civilization. "Ruled by powerful priests and warriors, they brought with them their male gods of war." Slowly, a new code—privileging the male— began to become imprinted in the mind of every individual, until their very concept of what is reality had been transformed to fit the requirements of the dominator society. Eisler writes:

"For millennia, one of the most important of these instruments of socialization was the 'spiritual education' carried out by the ancient priesthoods. As an integral part of state power, these priesthoods served, and were members of, the male elites who now everywhere ruled and exploited the people. The priests who now spread what they said was the divine Word—the Word of God that had magically been communicated to them were backed up by armies, courts of law, and executioners. The most powerful weapons were the 'sacred' stories, rituals, and priestly edicts through which they systematically inculcated in people's minds the fear of terrible, remote, and 'inscrutable' deities...A male-dominated, violent, and hierarchical society gradually began to be seen not only as normal, but also right."

Over the past several decades, there has been a grassroots movement—in scholarly, spiritual and political circles—to reclaim a partnership-based spirituality as the basis for an egalitarian society. It is too early in the history of humanity to judge whether such a movement can possibly stand up to all those who would harm rather than heal Eve—but every woman who personally breaks the ties that bind to toxic fundamentalism is simultaneously contributing to the possibility of a healthier world for those yet to come. One important reason for having a partnership society is that, in Eisler's words:

"The minds of children—both girls and boys—will no longer be fettered. It will be a world where limitation and fear will no longer be systematically taught us through myths about how inevitably evil and perverse we humans are...Our drive for justice, equality, and freedom, and our thirst for knowledge and spiritual illumination, and our yearning for love and beauty will at last be freed."

In the next chapter, we will revisit these themes once again, this time examining and offering specific guidance on how we can begin relating in healthier ways to the next generation of women—including our own daughters—to help them struggle towards self-respect, courage and freedom.

SPIRITUAL BEINGS

The partnership model is consistent with the concept of the actualized human being, as proposed by Abraham Maslow. These were but two of the many influences that inspired me to host a conference on the relationship among body, mind and spirit in New York City. One of the presenters was Detroit-based Unity minister, Reverend Karen Boland, who has now become a dear friend. I remember asking her opinion on Maslow's findings, which I referred to as "progression towards one's calling." Karen smiled appreciatively at the mention of Maslow, who had done so much to help provide scientific legitimacy to the notion of human beings advancing towards spirituality. But, she demurred modestly, she had adopted a different and even more promising belief system about human beings.

Karen believes that we all come to this earth with our spiritual qualities intact, and bring expression to them in human form. She went on to share her thinking that it is a shame that young students could not be taught at an early age that while, indeed, we are human beings, we contain a divine spark within us. Suddenly, it all clicked. Maslow's "peak experience" was no less than the out-breaking of that divine spark, connecting to something greater than us. Wayne Dyer used different words to say pretty much the same thing. We use our intuition to connect into the purpose that has been "in our hearts since birth" and express it in human form. If Karen and the other teachers are right, we come to this earth as spiritual beings knowing that we have a job to do in human form. If so, then the process of healing describes various ways to access our authentic selves, find our music, and play the music inside us that has been in our souls since birth. For those of us born or raised within religious fundamentalism, it would be purpose enough to break free from the prison of toxic beliefs and live however briefly in the intoxicating glory of spiritual freedom.

The bottom line is that we need no outside authority to connect us to God. We just need to access from within!

DYSFUNCTION CHECKLIST

From this perspective, it is not only possible but also natural to use our minds and hearts to seek out healthy spirituality and communities—and to identify and avoid the toxic ones. As I personally began to explore other spiritual options and organizations, I kept this handy checklist close at hand to remind myself what I was looking for: that which promised freedom and vitality rather than control and oppression. With this list, I could be in conversation with the past, transforming or transcending that which no longer served me. The list took the form of that from which I was definitively moving away and that to which I was inexorably being drawn:

1. *From God has all the power*
   to we are co-creators with God
2. *From sinfulness and punishment*
   to unconditional love and self-responsibility
3. *From men are superior to women*
   to we are equals
4. *From unquestionable truth*
   to the right to question
5. *From black and white thinking*
   to curiosity, tolerance and understanding
6. *From missionizing others*
   to encouraging self and individual responsibility

TAKING THE BEST

My research demonstrates that the women in my study, like me, have by and large felt free, at last, to establish a direct relationship with God that feels good and right to them. Interestingly enough, the vast majority of those surveyed explain that they did not reject fundamentalism due to its basic metaphysical assumptions—but rather, the interpretation. In more prosaic terms, few of us threw the baby out with the bath water.

Although I have rejected and replaced the toxic beliefs associated with the religion of my childhood and no longer buy into the Bible as being literally true, I do acknowledge the importance of some of its teachings. For example, there are moral guidelines for the conduct of human beings, such as the Golden Rule, that remain the cornerstone of my ethics. (As an aside, I have since learned that versions of the Golden Rule can be found in virtually every religion in the world.) As mentioned earlier, many of us—even the most damaged in our number—find ourselves turning to familiar scriptures for comfort. However, we no longer pray to the angry God to forgive our sinfulness. I have previously spoken of my fondness for the writings of Dr. Norman Vincent Peale who asserted that there is an inherent goodness in human beings. I also cannot say enough when it comes to voicing my gratitude for the liberation inherent in the words of Dr. Maxwell Maltz who helped me understand the importance of a positive self-image and visualization. Through him, I learned of the potential for spiritual discipline to work towards the attainment of one's dreams. Ironically, it was these brave interpreters of the same Bible that had enslaved my soul who now pointed the way toward freedom. Christianity has that potential to liberate us, as do all of the religions. However, none of our religions—even in their more spiritually evolved forms—holds the franchise on God. Over time, I have had the opportunity to study world religions and learned from the great masters of old, like the historical Jesus, Confucius, Buddha and Lao Tzu. Not one of them warned of hellfire and brimstone; none had a church. In fact, each taught that the individual had the capacity to connect with her or his source and to have a direct relationship with a power greater than we.

SPIRITUAL FREEDOM

Spiritual freedom allows us to explore the cornucopia of spiritual options that we can access once the authentic self is free to emerge. This newfound freedom has led the women in this book down many paths. Freed from what we see as "imposed" restrictions, the research participants have eagerly sought a passionate relationship to what most refer to simply as "spirit," creatively incorporating humanistic and eastern philosophy, alongside beliefs and practices from an abundance of sources, with uplifting traditional views and traditions.

Not all the participants have had an easy passage to a more meaningful relationship to spirit, however. Dottie had to go through a rehab center in order to find her authentic self. During her stay, she wrote a letter to a "Loving God," the one she remembered before Christian fundamentalism came into her life. She now prays directly to this loving God. Another former Christian fundamentalist, Adrian, loves to collect religious icons from around the world, but gives no power to them. Her only spiritual demonstrative act is a simple "Bless Us" before partaking in a meal. She gives credit to AA's 12-step program, starting with the acknowledgment that there is a Higher Power working in the world. However, it's her intuitive inner work that is giving her the messages on how to be more authentic. As diverse as is our spiritual expression, there is one thing we definitively share: the conviction to avoid religious dogma, at all costs.

In addition to the inspirational women you will meet in Part Four, we have some other wonderful, accessible role models of spiritual freedom in today's world. Maya Angelou and Oprah Winfrey, for example, have come to peaceful and healing resolutions of their oppressive upbringings. Religion was but one component of a complex family dynamic. Like most of the women in this book, they made a decision to retain remnants that they hold dear, but listen to their authentic selves as they express their spiritual freedom.

The melding of old and new is illustrated by something I recently wrote in my journal. Reflecting on what happened to me at the age of ten, verses in the Bible, Matthew 5:14–15, came to me.

Ye are the light of the world. A city that is set on a hill cannot be hid. Neither do men light a candle, and put it under a bushel, but on a candlestick; and it giveth light unto all that are in the house.

This scripture metaphorically refers to a person who allows her candle to be snuffed out and hidden under a bushel. That was my experience, entering into the fundamentalist Christian community at such an innocent age, feeling as though the light of my knowing had been snuffed out and had been taken over by outside authority figures. While journaling about the experience long ago I remembered the candlestick of light, and I suddenly understood that Matthew was encouraging us to be a candlestick that gives light to all who are in the house. This was not a threat—it was a promise. At last, I pictured myself as I believe Matthew intended: as the bearer of the inner light—my true birthright.

SPIRITUAL PRACTICES

Silence In the realm of spiritual freedom, there are no dogmas or requirements. However, there are practices you can follow to keep your relationship to your authentic self and to spirit present on a daily basis. The simplest is also the most effective. As I mentioned previously, every day, I take a few minutes to sit quietly. What then? I simply listen, turning inward for a new authority.

Perhaps you can set aside a special corner in your home where you place objects that remind you of who you are when you are feeling the spiritual connection between heart and universe. As I've suggested previously, there are many means by which to quiet your thoughts. You can write in your journal or meditate. At the very least, this will be precious time out of your busy life for contemplation of your soul's deeper yearnings. As you go deeper, you can pose to spirit a meaningful question and wait patiently for an answer to come to you. As you have the opportunity to test the validity of the messages you are receiving, you will become surer of your ability to receive directly the messages meant for you. Quieting the mind, asking the questions, waiting for answers is the path prescribed by many spiritual traditions as the means to realizing our authentic selves in this lifetime.

Transformative prayer Many of the participants also rely on one of the traditional modes of religious ritual: the power of the spoken word also known as "prayer." Even prayer can be refurbished when viewed through the creative lens of spirit. Esther and Jerry Hicks in *A New Beginning II* suggest that an effective prayer is to simply act as if what you want has already happened and allow the answers that will lead you to your goals to materialize. This is similar to the visualization practice recommended by Dr. Christine Northrup, cited earlier in this book. You can practice this prayer technique in conjunction with imagining a virtual reality in which you are already experiencing joy and happiness. As the authors point out, this new form of prayer is not about wishful thinking—it's about setting the stage for spirit to respond to the deepest behests of your heart.

The ultimate test These techniques, along with the journaling suggested earlier, can be utilized on a daily basis, both guiding you to explore the rich universe of spiritual possibilities—and preventing you from inadvertently falling back into outgrown systems of belief and practice. In *The Mythic Path*, Drs. Krippner and Feinstein provide a simple test concerning psychological health that can easily be adapted as a test for spiritual health, as well. Ask yourself: *Does your spirituality "usher you toward more fulfilling relationships, more rewarding social activities, greater social support, a present-centered absorption in the flow of life, physical fitness, and enough rest and personal solitude, all of which are also associated with happiness?"*

Answer these questions in the affirmative and you can trust that you are on a spiritual path that will lead you to the joy, peace and fulfillment you so richly deserve. You can keep the best of your religious upbringing, discard what no longer serves you and experiment with new, creative options trusting that after all you've been through, you can sort out the toxic from the life-giving. If you make a mistake, you can correct quickly and move on. In time, you will have a portfolio of beliefs and practices that support your authentic self: A place you will be free to call your true spiritual home.

CHAPTER EIGHT
Saving Our Children

Having read my life story—with its recurring themes of fear, perfectionism and shame—you will recognize the following vignette for the miracle it is. Recently, I was able to share part of this manuscript with my only child, Jack, a grown son with a family of his own. He reminded me that when he was in elementary school, I'd tried to find a non-denominational church for the two of us to attend. Remembering Dr. Norman Vincent Peale's positive thinking message and his integration of religion and psychology, I took Jack to a comparable church in Southern California. But having raised him to think for himself, Jack had already begun researching religion and spirituality on his own. In fact, in junior high school, he came home from the library with a stack of books to write a book report. When I asked him what it was about, he said "Zoroastrianism!" I had to go to the dictionary and look it up. Soon after, he became enthralled with the book *Siddhartha* by Herman Hesse. Our conversations over dinner were rich with commentary about eastern philosophy and its contribution to western thinking.

I enjoyed his open-mindedness, happy to support his choice to attend the University of San Francisco, a college taught not by Zoroastrians but by Jesuits—almost as radical a departure from the religion within which I was raised. During his university years, Jack's intellectual life continued to blossom, engaging in many open forums and debates with his professors on all religions. He loved the dialogue. During our recent phone call, after the reminiscing, I asked where he was in his belief system now? I could not help but feel a quiet joy in my heart when he told me that he is on a search for what he calls an unseen universal order. Is it physics, astrophysics, intuition, spirituality or a combination? He isn't ready to give it a name. Whatever he ends up calling it, I am pleased that Jack has retained the sense that we are not alone in a chaotic universe—but rather, that there is some sense to existence. I am even more pleased that he never had to fight off any of the demons I faced as a child. He did not go to bed at night dreading that he would have forgotten to confess every one of his sins before falling asleep, lest he die before morning. He did not have to visit neighbors at his parents' sides, convincing families with faiths of their own that lest they fall to their knees to take Jesus as their savior, they would be doomed to an eternity in hell. Whatever challenges life would bring his way—and what mistakes I might make in parenting—would, at any rate, not be metaphysically ordained, conscribed by the dictates of an unassailable authority. If either of us ever fell short of the quest for perfectionism that had been my family's legacy, there was at the very least compassion and forgiveness—and not just between us and God, but between each other, mere human beings doing our best.

NOT OUR CHILDREN

All of the women whose stories I share in this book have concerns about not wanting to pass on the dysfunction of fundamentalism to their children. As described by many of the women in my research study, daughters raised in fundamentalist households are taught to believe that to earn the love of God, they must live with the fear of sinning, going to hell or becoming ostracized, and not ever being good enough. But it's not only the girls who are affected. Sons, too, adopt rigid beliefs about right and wrong, forced to trade in their inquisitive minds for black and white thinking. For some of the women I interviewed, the pain has been so great, they have foregone having children entirely. Taught at an early age about the innate depravity of human beings, the Native American in my research study, Teresa, remembers a Christian hymn that forced her to admit that she was a but a "worm." Many of the interviewees remember being taught to sing songs in which they confessed to being a "wretch." The words affected them to the point that they had a hard time keeping themselves on a positive track, let alone bringing a child into this environment. "How do you stop the constant mindset? It still affects your decisions today, and your moods, and how you feel about yourself. How could I not pass that along to the next generation, even if I tried my hardest not to?" one of them poignantly commented, a refrain I heard, sadly, many times.

For others in the research group, children were born after the break from fundamentalism, allowing the mother a fresh slate to help her offspring get it right from the start. In many instances, however, children were born into fundamentalism and in some cases, continue to be split between one parent who escaped from rigid religious, spiritual or psychological communities and that parent's spouse who is still involved. Even among those who have personally foregone the joy of parenting, the majority of us believe that it is both our task and our privilege to gently guide the next generation to establish a healthy relationship to spirituality. In some cases, this relationship is forged within more liberal interpretations of the religion within which their parent had been raised. For others, like Jack, spirituality has become a path with unexpected twists and turns.

IMPORTANT RESEARCH

How can we relate to the next generation of children—including our own sons and daughters—to help them minimize or avoid entirely the energy-consuming battles that their mothers have had to mount to win our own spiritual freedom? In this chapter, I share with you the latest research drawn from the fields of psychology and religious education both in terms of undoing the damage that has already been inflicted and of suggesting some healthier methods and expectations by which to raise our children. This is no small issue. Paraphrasing Eli S. Chesen, M.D. from his helpful book, *Religion May be Hazardous to Your Health*: people who are not embedded within religion will look at life and ask questions like "Who am I?" "How did I get here?" "How should I live?" "Where am I going?" "Why am I going there?" and "Where am I going after I have been there?" Individuals growing up in a community of true believers will not have found it necessary or even possible to think through these questions to their own satisfaction and "therefore shall have learned nothing" about themselves.

Not only is it imperative that children learn about themselves—as well as their parents' and the larger society's beliefs—but that they do so at age-appropriate junctures. Psychologists and educators have developed theories based on empirical research that demonstrate how our educational institutions—including religious schools and programming—can work with parents to create the healthiest rather than most toxic environment for the cultivation of dynamic children. Since the influence of the developmental psychologists, the thinking has centered on stage theory targeting appropriate levels and types of instructions for groups of children sorted by age.

In the stage theory model, the teaching that occurs at the earliest ages—prior to age five—becomes critically important. The reason for this is that the child's earliest environmental influences create the lens through which he or she will view the world. Religious dogma has the effect of becoming a rigid "failsafe," a learned rigidity that precludes objective thinking and respect for one's own intuitions. Writes Chesen: "This (failsafe) mechanism is a very necessary component of the rigid thinker's mind: without it he is vulnerable to new concepts, and these might threaten his stereotyped way of thinking and upset his dogmatic applecart."

A child raised in this way may appear to be thinking for him or herself—but in actuality, the child is doing little more than repeating dogma, or coming up with his or her own variations within consciously or unconsciously prescribed boundaries. Tampering fundamentally with received knowledge is forbidden and as many of our stories illustrate, even healthy questioning is met with repercussions to the child.

Another reason the early stages of education are so important is that abstract religious concepts, when taught to a child at an inappropriately young age, will be misunderstood and wrongly interpreted. Even at age ten, I could only parrot my request for salvation and go through the motions of presenting myself to the minister for immersion in the baptismal waters. The reality is that I had little to no understanding of the theological significance of the activity, and experienced it only as punishment for having been born.

The important thing to note is that the psychologists or educators quoted in this chapter do not automatically think that religion or religious education are wrong or bad, in and of themselves. They do, however, prescribe a way to share a community's beliefs and practices that are respectful of the child's capabilities and potential. Chesen, in a wonderful chapter titled "How to Teach your Children a Healthy Attitude about Religion: A Parent's Guide," summarizes educational building blocks that parents and teachers should consider when selecting or creating religious school programming. In brief, here are highlights from three stages, enhanced and supported by the thinking of other educators and psychologists who are supportive of Chesen's prescription.

STAGE ONE (BIRTH TO AGE SIX)

In this early stage, abstract thoughts are beyond the grasp of the child's immature thought processes. Salvation, God, heaven and hell, for example, will not be adequately understood. This stage, therefore, precludes formal religious education centering on conceptual work. But even metaphorical stories, such as the creation story in Genesis, can only be understood concretely as fact. This will cause the child problems down the line when she is introduced to evolutionary theory in elementary school.

Rather than confuse the child or lay a basis for future problems, the educators suggest that simple, concrete religious rituals that create a warm sense of well being and community are more age-appropriate. The teaching and singing of Christmas carols, lighting candles and the like will be appreciated by the young child, setting the stage for a positive feeling about religion that can begin to blossom in stage two.

STAGE TWO (AGES SIX TO TWELVE)

This is the appropriate age for the initiation of formal religious education. In the beginning years of this stage, hands-on experiences are still more effective, such as introducing prayer to the children by taking them to religious services. As the child begins to master abstract thinking, the child is now able to process such concepts as God and death, and to understand the metaphorical nature of Bible stories. Even so, the educator and parent will want to avoid rote teaching of Biblical concepts as law. For instance, not all of the Ten Commandments—such as injunctions against adultery—are appropriate even in the latter portion of this stage. When introducing abstract concepts—such as God—the parent/educator should be willing to encourage each child to feel free to question the concepts being introduced without fear of retribution. In fact, the teacher should be free to share his or her own questions, as well.

STAGE THREE (AGES THIRTEEN AND OVER)

If the child has been educated age-appropriately, this final stage will comprise both the most challenging and rewarding period for educators and parents. It is in Stage Three that the young adult turns into an independent thinker, with all the positive and negative ramifications that this implies. In the words of psychologist Erik Erikson, during this stage of late adolescence:

> "No longer is it merely for the old to teach the young the meaning of life. It is the young who, by their responses and actions, tell the old whether life as represented to them has some vital promise, and it is the young who carry in them the power to confirm those who confirm them to renew and regenerate, to disavow what is rotten, or reform and rebel."

This is perceived by Erikson and many psychologists and educators as not only something that is normal for adolescents to undergo— but vital for the good of society.

Teresa, while not having children of her own, has taken her job as an educator seriously, working with children at all three stages to rectify the toxic fundamentalism within which she was raised. When I visited her for our formal interview, I saw a vital woman, surrounded by adoring nephews and nieces who freely came in and out of her adobe home. While they visited, she was equally comfortable teaching them songs in their native Tewa language as she was in sharing with them the warmth of Christmas gift-exchange, one Christian ritual that she still relishes as a reflection of

God's love. She has taken the best of both her religious belief systems and has taught the next generation by example to keep an open mind and heart. She has even somewhat countered her resentment of her fundamentalist upbringing by giving credit to, if nothing else, the fundamentalist influence of the value of education. With her doctorate of sociology in hand, she teaches tolerance, freedom of thought and mutual respect to her students in community college.

OURSELVES—OUR CHILDREN

Women who have found spiritual freedom for themselves are surprisingly well equipped to understand the residues of fundamentalism experienced by their own children, including those whose beginnings took root in fundamentalist soil. For these children, anger, fear and shame are three of the negative emotions that must be addressed.

Anger is a particularly challenging emotion for children raised in Christian fundamentalism, reflecting the fact that they have been caught in a confusing intellectual and psychological paradox. On the one hand, the children are taught that God is an angry, vengeful God, actively punishing those who sin. However, the last thing these very same children are permitted by fundamentalist Christianity to experience is anger, either toward God, or toward others. Anger toward God is punishable by being sent to hell for eternity. The Christian fundamentalist child is not permitted to have an angry attitude toward the unfairness of God, for example, for sending good people to suffer in hell for no reason other than their unbelief. At the same time, anger toward other individuals is prohibited by Christian fundamentalism inasmuch as this is considered tantamount to murdering these individuals. In fact, the idea of "turning the other cheek" was encouraged by the church (Luke 6:27-29).

The pressure on the child to suppress his or her own anger, as well as any of the other healthy but forbidden emotions that fundamentalism considers undesirable, bears consequences. Alice Miller, in *For Your Own Good: Hidden Cruelty in Child-Rearing and the Roots of Violence* describes the powerful, negative emotions experienced by children who are forced to conform to the pedagogy or agenda imposed by adults. According to Miller, the child's own impulses and feelings are denied and suppressed, and if the child's reaction to this unfair treatment is not expressed, the child will learn to remain silent. "This silence is a sign of the effectiveness of the pedagogical principles applied, but at the same time it is a danger signal pointing to future pathological development." Miller terms this "poisonous pedagogy," and the result is that the child's self-concept will suffer.

As recovering fundamentalists—brave mothers healing from prohibitions against anger themselves—can use the Healing Eve process to break the silence and recover access to their own true emotions. One of the participants, Dottie, shared the story of a breakthrough moment with me. Some years previously, Dottie had put herself on the road to recovery, having come to recognize that addiction to painkillers had become a self-destructive rebellion against her fundamentalist upbringing. She put herself into drug rehabilitation, doing the hard work of breaking free from reactivity to spiritual freedom. In particular, she remembered one momentous day soon after leaving rehab when her parents were visiting with her and her two children at her home. When one of the children spilled her drink on the light-colored carpets, her father automatically scolded the little girl: "Shame on you!" Dottie recoiled at those words, and shocked her father with her bold reply. "I don't want to ever hear those words in this house again." At that moment, Dottie realized that she had spontaneously left the vengeful God behind and embraced a belief in a loving God. "And the most important part of this is that I knew that God loves me and my children enough to allow us to own our own appropriate anger," says Dottie.

Another participant, Robin, overheard her visiting mother talking to her two young sons, shortly after Robin's divorce to an abusive husband. The mother had just gotten out the first sentence: "You boys need to know that your mother is going to burn in hell forever, while you two are going to heaven." Without skipping a beat, Robin burst in: "You stop that right now! Don't you ever, ever say that to my children again, or you will never see them again." Robin refuses to expose her sons to the angry Christian interpretation of God, instead sharing the wonders of nature as the most direct and healthy path to a spiritual life, saying: "I don't want done to my children what was done to me."

Ironically, encouraging the healthy expression of anger in our children is equally important to establishing the notion of a loving, forgiving God. Says Philip Greven, author of *Spare the Child: The Religious Roots of Punishment and the Psychological Impact of Physical Abuse* (1991):

> "Anger is a child's best (and often only) defense, for it arises out of a powerful sense of self, a self being violated and abused by painful blows and hurtful words. The child has been hurt on purpose by an adult in order to teach a lesson in discipline, but the child experiences this pain and reproach as an assault upon the self as well as upon the body."

FEAR AND PUNISHMENT

Walking hand-in-hand with anger is the negative impact of unhealthy forms of punishment. Many of the research participants cited the use of one of the Proverbs as justification that had been used against them for punishment in childhood.

Withhold not correction from the child: for if thou beatest him with the rod, he shall not die. Thou shalt beat him with the rod, and shalt deliver his soul from hell.

PROVERBS (23:13-14)

Contemporary psychological research demonstrates unequivocally that corporal punishment dehumanizes a child. Christian psychiatrist, D. Ross Campbell sees many children who are strictly disciplined, but feel unloved. Parenting expert Benjamin Spock, early on an advocate of physical discipline, changed his advice over the years and began taking a stand against the practice of corporal punishment. In his 1985 edition of *Baby Care and Parenting*, Spock explained:

"There are several reasons to try to avoid physical punishment, I feel. It teaches children that the larger, stronger person has the power to get his way, whether or not he is in the right, and they may resent this in their parent for life. Some spanked children feel quite justified in beating up on smaller ones."

Equally toxic is excessive moralizing. Hugh Missildine, M.D., in his book *Your Inner Child of the Past*, suggests that some of the most punitive parents can proudly declare that they "never laid" a hand on their child. Instead, they set up black and white rules of conduct that pose artificially rigid standards by which children are to be judged. When the child falls short or rebels, the authorities are quick to label even age-appropriate behavior "bad" and "evil." Missildine writes that, in fact, "many children will tell you it is harder to bear—for the punishment immediately becomes self-punishment and may be carried on endlessly by the child within himself. Much moralizing creates a profound self-belittling distortion in the child's feeling about himself."

Reviewing the themes of guilt, shame and worthlessness that run all too prevalently throughout the stories shared in this book, I realized that for daughters raised in Protestant fundamentalism, in particular, we had much more to deal with than the official Ten Commandments. None of us disagree with prohibitions against killing, for instance. But here are just ten of the real commandments that were regularly enforced to punitive effect.

THE PROTESTANT FUNDAMENTALIST DAUGHTER'S
TOP TEN COMMANDMENTS

1. Thou shalt not have impure thoughts,
   let alone premarital sex.
2. Thou shalt wear no finger or toenail polish
   and as for make-up and short hair, forget about it.
3. Thou shalt not dance, drink or smoke.
4. Thou shalt have no association with non-Christians,
   unless for the purpose of proselytizing.
5. Thou shalt not question authority.
6. Thou shalt not wear shorts.
7. Thou shalt not divorce even an abusive husband.
8. Thou shalt not hold a position of power in the church.
9. Thou shalt not play cards, go to see secular television
   or movies or read any book not approved by
   one's church.
10. Thou shalt not have *self-esteem*.

Whether physical or emotional, psychologists and educators have by and large come to agree that punitiveness is not an effective teaching tool in the long run. In fact, excessive force creates a backlash in the child, whose real thoughts and feelings go deeply underground in a volatile stew of self-hatred and resentment. I will revisit this issue in the conclusion, where I will address the growing violence among youth in our global community—be it suicide bombers, terrorists, mass murderers or young people bent on self-destruction. As you already know, this is no small issue and the urgency of this situation must be addressed. As women and mothers, we can do more than we have been taught to think we can. We can break the patterns of shame, guilt, resentment, anger and fear. The place to start is in our own families.

CORRECTING MID-STREAM

Even if you were raised in this milieu of rigid authoritarianism yourself—and even if you have already consciously or inadvertently passed some of the damage on to your own children—it's not too late to short-circuit the toxic patterns and take steps to create a healthier relationship to yourself and your offspring. Interestingly enough, correcting the destructive patterns of the past begins not with your children—but with yourself. If you have done the exercises in Part Two, you are already well on your way to healing your children, as well. If you can love, accept and forgive yourself, you are less likely to judge your children harshly. If you can see your own worthiness—your own strengths and contributions—and if you can forgive your imperfections, you will see your children's worthiness, strengths and contributions, as well. You will be a role model to them, showing them the healing power of self-love.

You are already learning how to offer yourself the approval you were denied as a child. You can now embrace your own inner child, and become a loving parent to yourself. This includes replacing punitive self-talk with heart-felt self-acceptance. Hugh Missildine has some wonderful phrases that I have found most helpful. The first is something you can say to yourself when you feel the urge to react angrily—either against yourself or your children: *"Yes, I'm really burned up, but a lot of this hate and furious resentment is simply my inner child of the past raging over past punishments I didn't deserve. But part of this is self-punishment. I am not going to fly off the handle, saying and doing things that are going to result in more punishment and hostility just to satisfy these past resentments. This isn't that much of an issue. That is the way I acted before. I do not have to be a punitive parent to myself."*

There will certainly be times when even armed with this powerful self-talk, you do something for which you feel guilty or ashamed. This phrase can be used in regards to a wide range of transgressions—real or imagined—including regret over the things you have done to your children: *"That guilty feeling and self-belittling was created in my childhood and doesn't belong to my activities and life today. I am not going to beat myself up about that mistake but correct it and try to be more careful."*

I do not want to make this sound easier than it is. At first, you may find yourself needing to say these phrases to yourself many times a day, living your new life of self-love one hour, one minute, one second at a time. One of the study participants, Mary, has had to face mountains of regret for having raised her two daughters in

Christian fundamentalism. They were teenagers before she finally saw the hypocrisy of the church community and left. She now follows the premise that all human beings have a divine spark, refusing to become involved in any kind of organized religion. Instead, she practices yoga with an instructor who is helping her bring healing energy to not only her body but also her mind and spirit. She has had to do so despite terrible odds. Mary remains close to one of her daughters, now in her early twenties. They are able to speak openly about the generations of pain inflicted upon them both and have come to support one another to healthier relationships to spirituality—and to each other. Sadly, the other daughter has disowned Mary and barred her from seeing her grandchildren because she is no longer a practicing Christian fundamentalist. Working at it moment by moment, Mary holds all her children and grandchildren in loving thoughts and waits patiently for her daughter to soften the rigidity of her position, in which Mary knows she played a contributing role.

While it is difficult for Mary, she understands that recovery from fundamentalism requires the unconditional surrendering of coercive measures. She could not force her daughter to leave fundamentalism, even if she wanted to. She has also come to understand that the road to health for her, as well, requires the reduction of both regrets and "shoulds" in her life. You may recall in an earlier chapter my first encounter with Manuel J. Smith's *Bill of Assertive Rights*. In his book, *When I Say No, I Feel Guilty*, he taught me to replace the notion of "I should" or "I have to" with "If I like" or "If I don't like." In Dr. Smith's words, *I learned that I have the right to judge my own behavior, thoughts, and emotions and to take the responsibility for their initiation and consequences upon myself. I have the right to offer no reasons or excuses for justifying my behavior and I have the right to say 'No'.* Mary did not have to like her daughter's rejection—but she did not have to give up her own newfound happiness in life, either.

Missildine writes: "As you begin to find satisfaction in your ability to act without coercive threats to yourself, your resistance will further decrease and your confidence and ability to act will grow."

Missildine has come up with a wonderful list of correctives in regards to toxic childhood patterns, which I have adapted for our specific purpose.

- When you are concerned about your or your child's falling short of your high ideals, you can today reduce the pressure and lower the demands, which you put on yourself and your offspring.
- In place of punitiveness, you can extend kindness and gentleness to yourself and your child, limiting your self-criticism.
- If you were raised in an overly submissive manner— and have the tendency to impose your will on your children—you can self-correct by paying more attention to respecting the feelings and rights of all concerned, including yourself.
- In place of neglect, you can perform kindnesses.

Missildine's correctives demonstrate that there are many interpretations of "reality." When we take the hardest line against our children, and ourselves we are misjudging that reality— replacing a loving and kind worldview with an interpretation of "truth" that is harsh and unforgiving. By trading a punitive reality for a loving one, I no longer was doomed to pass along to my child the dysfunctional theology within which I was raised. I am not alone. Later you will hear the story of Carmen, one of women in the research group who found it within her heart to call upon nearly super-human courage to shield her son from his fundamentalist grandmother's toxic agenda. Standing up to her mother's negative judgments about her loving, non-punitive parenting, she had made up her mind to refuse her mother further access to her son. This takes guts!

FURTHER ASSISTANCE
If you have read this far in this book and still find the task of breaking the ties that bind to be daunting, you may be a candidate for psychological counseling. Many of the women in the research study sought out and benefited from an educated outside perspective.

In addition to psychological counseling, many of the women—as discussed in the previous chapter—have received support, clarity and hope from their spiritual involvements. While definitively turning their backs on fundamentalist doctrine, many have established a direct relationship to a power greater than themselves.

You may recall my prescription for transformational prayer. My concept was influenced by the wise and influential advice of Florence Scovel Shinn in her 1920s classic *The Game of Life and How to Play It*. In it, Shinn instructs mothers not to send their children out the door with any fearful or negative utterances. "Rather, one should speak in positive terms to their children; and their prayers should contain a positive attitude that their children will be divinely protected." Regardless of how dim things may look at any given moment in time, there is always hope.

THE HEALTHY CHILD

This chapter ends, then, on a positive note: envisioning what is possible for our children and for our children's children. Adapting his words to address our daughters, as we support them towards a spiritually healthy adulthood, here is what Chesen's research describes: The healthy youth will need flexibility and adaptability as she approaches and masters new kinds of work and meets and deals with all kinds of people. In order to take on the many challenges of the fully lived life, she must be able to move beyond the impediment of baseline prejudices dating back to childhood. Her thinking abilities logically extend further if they are not closed in by boundary lines and ill-founded taboos. As this youth grows into a healthy adult, she will be able to enjoy living and can continue doing so, and not at the expense of others. She is able to derive independent happiness as well as interdependent happiness. Moreover, she is able to tolerate reasonably stressful situations, should they arise. Finally, she is able to set and achieve reasonable goals and to interact successfully with people while enroute to her goals.

In its own way, this does not seem too much to ask. On the other hand, it is everything.

PART FOUR

Healing the Wounded Eve
Three Research Participants
Share their Stories

✳✳✳✳✳✳

CHAPTER NINE

Teresa: Healing Shame

At The Cross
Alas and did my Savior bleed and did my Sov'reign die?
Would he devote that sacred head for such a worm as I?
TRADITIONAL CHRISTIAN HYMN,
as taught to Teresa by the missionaries
at her reservation, circa 1950s

In the introduction, I shared with you the emotional experience of being greeted by the research participant Teresa in her adobe home. She had taken in my coiffed blond hair and carefully-selected outfit with a look of horror on her face, my appearance having inadvertently reminded her of the missionary sisters who had come to that same front stoop many years ago. This was not the first time we'd met, but our previous encounter was on a tour of archeological sites. She was the guide, I the student—and we were both dressed in blue jeans and covered with red dust from head to toe.

Riding in the back of her van, chatting busily with my fellow students between sites, I marveled at myself, that Jimmy Laura Smull, the little girl who had been raised on creationism, was now engaged in anthropological research. As I drifted in and out of my classmates' conversations, I inwardly paid homage to the real estate license that had opened a window of freedom in my mind. In the years since my break with the church community, I had moved quickly and steadily through introductory courses at a local junior college, a B.A. and M.A. in anthropology, including coursework in archeology, at California State Fullerton and now, I was doing field research for my doctorate in human sciences at Saybrook Research and Graduate School. Drifting in and out of the conversation as my friends compared thoughts about the sites we had visited, my eyes suddenly caught a glimpse of the tour guide looking at me inquisitively in her rear view mirror.

"I heard you were working toward a Ph.D. What is your subject matter?" She politely inquired. While I had been following her around all day, I realized that aside from the wealth of information she had been sharing with us about her Native American subject matter, I knew nothing more about her than her name and title. She was Dr. Teresa Willow, a sociologist from the local junior college. She wore her hair in a beautiful, thick braid laced with shades of gray and white, flowing down her sturdy back. Despite the fact that we seemed to be about the same age, I assumed that the academic connection and our dusty jeans were about all we had in common. Nevertheless, I explained to her my particular area of interest: stories of women—like me—who had broken free from Christian fundamentalism.

"Oh boy," Teresa exclaimed, startling all of us with her intensity. "Have I got a story for you!"

CONNECTION

From that moment on, the visits to the Native American sites on our formal agenda took back seat for me as Teresa began to share her personal story: a story that offered startling parallels as well as discomfiting differences with my own. As it turns out, Teresa and I are exactly the same age. More startling, at precisely the same tender stage in life, we had each been thrown into all-encompassing milieus of repression, rigidity, fear and anger delivered to us in the guise of Christianity. In fact, it was probable that the missionaries who came to Sunday school class in our wealthy church in Texas to collect our bundles of hand-me-down clothing had carried them to the remote reservation that Teresa called home. Teresa explained, her voice shaking with emotion, that while the missionaries promised her a religion and culture superior to her own, what they delivered to her was, in truth, little more than a sense of her own shame. I wanted to hear everything, but too soon, the tour ended. As Teresa and I parted company, she gave me her home phone number and an invitation to continue the conversation over a pot of tea at her adobe home the next time I was in the vicinity of her reservation. Her use of the word "shame" had sent shivers down my spine. As soon as I got home, I looked it up in the dictionary.

> "Shame: 1. A painful feeling of having done something wrong, improper, or silly. 2. A loss of reputation; disgrace, dishonor. 3. A fact to be sorry about; circumstance that brings disgrace, dishonor, or regret; pity." *World Book Dictionary, 17th edition*

I completely resonated with Teresa's emphasis on the heavily packed word "shame" and I knew that our much-anticipated meeting would be an important one for me.

We met again, some months later, in Teresa's adobe home—600 square feet on the edge of the reservation, less than one mile away from the house in which she'd been born. Proudly, she gave me a tour. Here was the indoor bathroom she'd just put in, after years of sharing an outhouse with others. Here was the insulation she'd installed herself. Here, too, were artifacts from the richly lived life: handmade gifts of clay and yarn given to her by her nieces and nephews. Sacramental objects, too, adorned her humble dwelling. There were feathered rattles and woven dream catchers. We settled before the potbelly stove, the sounds of pigs, sheep and children just outside the open door. Teresa looked completely at home in this world. As the day progressed and her story unfolded, I realized that this was no less than a miracle. This is Teresa's story.

THE BREATH

Teresa was born into a large extended family, rich with tradition. Growing up, she would sit for hours listening to stories about her Great-grandmother, the community herbalist, healer and midwife named for the supernatural source of their tribe's food staple, Mother Corn. Mother Corn only knew the English alphabet up to the letter "e," but she was the keeper of detailed information about the ceremonial seasonal cycle—and most importantly, about the Breath.

"We were taught that we lived in a world where all things are alive: the trees, rocks, mountains, clouds, all of those things were very vital, and we took these things in through what we called the Breath."

The exchange of sacred Breath set up a rhythm of reciprocation. If a deer or swan gave up its life for the people, the community honored the animal's spirit with a special ceremonial dance. Gratitude and reciprocity were extended to the least of the creatures. Not even a "worm" was a nothing—a symbol of shame and unworthiness—in Teresa's early world. There was an earthiness, in Teresa's words, a "femininity" that animated the super-natural spirits of her world.

Not that life on the reservation was easy. Teresa knew that her family was dirt poor. With five brothers and sisters, she watched her mother struggle to feed and clothe the children, often at her own expense. Her father wasn't any help, spending most of his paycheck on liquor. Teresa remembered times when he would come home from a weekend drunken brawl, only to pick a violent fight with her mother. Teresa remembers her mother hurriedly waking the children in the middle of the night and sending them to run to their grandmother's house for protection.

THE MISSIONARIES' PROMISE

Her family's situation was growing desperate, just as two spinster missionaries from Texas arrived at the reservation. When the missionaries knocked at her door, bearing gifts of food and clothing, and promising more, her mother let them in. The price was high, however. Teresa's family was told that they must leave their old ways behind and accept Jesus as their savior. In the missionaries' salvation package, Jesus did not stand alone as the source of religious promise but rather came bundled with a culture of rigid rules of conduct that somehow connected every detail of ordinary life to salvation. In the words of John Bradshaw, author of the book *Healing the Shame that Binds You*, life was now meant to follow a "religious script."

"There is a religious script, which contains the standards of holiness and righteous behavior. These standards dictate how to talk (there is a proper God voice), how to dress, walk and behave in almost every situation. Departure from this standard is deemed sinful."

To Teresa, accepting Jesus meant giving up everything she valued in her life and replacing it with the values, rules and practices of Christian fundamentalism. Earlier, I shared the story of the day Teresa watched her mother return home from her first shopping trip with her new missionary friends, her traditional hand-beaded dress in a paper bag. In its place, her mother had been squeezed into a corset, little white gloves and a pillbox hat. For Teresa, the abhorrent corset symbolized a regimentation foreign to the Native American culture: a day that was now rigidly compartmentalized into Sunday school classes, Sunday and Wednesday services, girl's club meetings, "good deeds" and more. Fundamentalism took over her life, taking away her freedom of movement and management over her own time. Even summers, Teresa and her siblings were taken to a Baptist encampment in the mountains at which the children were totally immersed in a Christian regimen of prayers, study and never-ending confession.

CONVERSION

The missionaries worked over Teresa's extended family, looking for converts. This was not an easy task, as anybody who had food on their table could easily resist taking on the rigid rules that played the leading role following conversion. There were a couple of uncles and aunts who signed on, along with Teresa's mother and the six children. But the biggest prize of all was the conversion of her father. Even what might have seemed to outsiders to be a good thing—the conversion of her father away from alcohol and into the church—was experienced by Teresa as a loss. Certainly, her father's violent fanaticism remained undiminished: but now, instead of alcohol as the subject of his desire, the watchword was "salvation." Pleasing the missionaries no end, Teresa's father was sent to a summer program at their seminary in California to become a Baptist mission minister. After several months' training, he returned to the reservation and set to work building a church right in the middle of the reservation. With the help of his extended family, he laid each one of the adobe bricks into the structure, building his church one brick at a time. He assumed that it wouldn't be long before all 500 plus of the reservation community converted. However, under her father's heavy hand—coupled with his swift and shallow training—the church became little more than a pulpit for his personal grievances. Wielding his newfound power, Reverend Willow watched his family's behavior closely. If his wife were caught singing a traditional song before slaying a chicken, she would become the subject of that day's hellfire and brimstone sermon. The children dreaded coming to the many services at church even a few minutes late, knowing that they, too, would be offered up as the sermon of the day.

SHOWCASE

Equally abhorrent were the visits from outsiders to her father's church and even their family home, where the missionaries put Teresa and her family on display. With a lethal mixture of pride and pity, the missionaries showed off to donors to the Missionary Outreach Program how well the "heathens" had been Christianized. "There was no consideration for our privacy. Whenever there was a knock on the door, I would hide in the closet until they left." Viewing their modest circumstances as an occasion for pity, the well-groomed visitors would write out checks to fund the spinster missionaries' work. "It was all so undignified." While the missionaries turned her father's church into a showcase, Teresa mourned. The more the missionaries taught her about Jesus Christ, the greater the loss she felt. After all, she had been born into a feminine world.

"Then all of a sudden, you've got this male deity and the point of anything and everything is about working upwards. What happened to my loving, reciprocating earth? For me, it was all so amazingly male. It's the male that becomes a supernatural and the woman takes on the burden of shame, and I wonder: *How come that happened?*"

When Teresa got to this part of her story, both she and I felt tears welling up. I recalled the horror I felt when told that Eve, by biting into the forbidden fruit, had brought sin into the world. Teresa was equally upset when she read the part in the scriptures about Eve being taken from the rib of Adam.

*"And the Lord God caused a deep sleep to fall upon Adam,
and he slept; and he took one of his ribs, and closed up the flesh
instead, thereof...And from the rib, which the Lord God
had taken from man, made he a woman,
and brought her unto the man."*
GENESIS (2:21–22)

As the missionaries interpreted the gospel, women were not created to stand-alone but rather to be subservient to the man, who was the source—the head—of the Christian community on earth. "When I am born into this Christian fundamentalism, I am told that I am a woman, that Eve brought sin on the world. Because I am a woman, I am going to continue this sinfulness." Suddenly, Teresa was taught she needed the authority of a man over her to keep her evil tendencies at bay. The irony of this is that prior to the missionaries' arrival, it had been the women in Teresa's life who had been the spiritual leaders. "The earth, itself, had been feminine: the embodiment of sharing and generosity, respect and self-sacrifice. And then, to be told that we, as women, were born particularly sinful. How is that a good way to start living your life: guilty and ashamed?" In a later chapter, you will get to know another one of my co-researchers, Adrian. Adrian would have felt right at home in our conversation when she commented to me: "The first thing I knew about myself was that I made a big mistake being female, and I shouldn't have done that."

A NEW KIND OF ABUSE

Teresa wept: "It was bad enough that my mother had been abused by her alcoholic husband for years. But now, there was another kind of abuse: suddenly, she was not good enough as she was." Teresa remembers one particularly painful incident—her father screaming at her mother because she didn't know how to bake a cookie. "The missionaries told her husband that church wives bake chocolate chip cookies to hand out after services. Mother could make wonderful old-fashioned foods like deer venison stews: cut up the deer, make it real. But she felt ashamed because she couldn't bake a stupid cookie."

It was Teresa's father who had been the alcoholic. But nevertheless, among his favorite themes was resisting the temptation of the "wicked world" outside of fundamentalism. Encouraged by the missionary establishment, Reverend Willow could, and did, rail for hours on end against a return to the lusts of the flesh.

For it had been better for them not to have known the way of righteousness, than, after they have known it, to turn from the holy commandment delivered unto them.
II PETER (2:21)

The "wicked world" now referred to anything that had to do with the 500 plus in the community who resisted joining her father's church. "All of the joys of my childhood—the reciprocity, the Breath—was something to be left behind because now you were a born-again Christian. Even at eight years of age, I knew there was something off about all this. If I ever wanted to go with my old friends and do a corn dance or sing a traditional song, as I had been doing all my life, the missionaries would accuse me of blasphemy: an affront to God. I just couldn't swallow that there was anything wrong with the rituals performed in the kivas. Was I ready to suddenly give up the belief in the super-naturals who came to replenish the community and its people? Who were these outsiders to tell us that what was happening within our community was bad? This was my birthright. How could this be a sin?"

Despite all the talk about damnation that filled her church life, it wasn't hell that frightened her. "There is a wisdom in the old way of thinking that is far superior to something that asks you to forsake your life here on earth for an afterlife. Taking the Breath is here and now: the more you take the Breath of all things around you, the better the human being you are. On the other hand, the promise of salvation is about denying the present for an imagined future. I never bought the concept of heaven and hell: that wasn't what scared me." Rather, what Teresa feared most was the missionaries.

BURIED BY SHAME

While the eight-year-old Teresa resisted feeling shame about her traditional beliefs, the missionaries were not to be deterred. They burrowed deeply beneath her skin, until the concept of her own inferiority had been insinuated into her very bones. Teresa bitterly remembers a meeting of the Christian girl's club at the missionaries' home.

"When I was young, I suffered from what I now have come to understand were mild epileptic seizures. I experienced them as fainting spells, my breath making a kind of whistling noise as I went under. I was already extremely self-conscious about these episodes when six of us were invited to the missionaries' home for a meeting of the Girl Ambassadors. Partway through the session, I felt one of these spells coming on. The next thing I remember is waking up, the elder of the two missionaries, who wore her hair braided and tied up tight in a crown on the top of her head, bending over me. She looked severe, wearing no make-up and a high-necked dress. I longed to be comforted but instead, as soon as she saw I was awake, she stood bold upright and proclaimed before the assembled group: 'I always knew there was something odd about you.' I remember thinking that there would never be a way to build a bridge between me and someone like this missionary who could take something as sensitive as this and turn it into ridicule."

OSTRACIZED

But by then, ridicule had become an everyday fact in Teresa's life. When Teresa and her family converted, the reservation community, who by and large viewed Baptism as selling out, had ostracized them. While her father busied himself building his church in the center of the reservation, Teresa and her siblings continued to attend the government school that served their reservation. Only now, they would have rocks thrown at them by the same kids who used to be their friends. In retrospect, Teresa realizes that her friends took her new time-consuming involvements—the very things she detested— as personal rejection. But it wasn't only her schoolmates who ostracized her and her family. "They called us 'those Borte,' which was their denigrating name for Baptists. After 51 years, many of the

Indians in this community still look at our family members as outsiders." They were and continue to be marginalized by the reservation, Teresa's family giving up the embrace of their own community. Unfortunately, it was not replaced with the loving Christian community they'd been promised.

"I think these two old maid missionaries sincerely wanted to upgrade our lives by providing us with food and used clothes, but as far as treating us so that we didn't feel inferior always—that never happened. It wasn't really Christian love that came through to us. It was pity. They would pick us up for church camp and school, but always out of a sense of moral superiority. We went obediently, but we never fit in. Proselytizing is unforgivable because it takes away one's sense of comfort in the world, a sense of self, a sense of confidence that is private, intimate, and replaces it with something inauthentic that comes from outside yourself. If you're already self-conscious, you're made to feel more self-conscious. You can't live in your own environment anymore because you're always feeling less than. You feel less than the missionaries, less than your old friends, ashamed about what you really believe and who you really are."

BAPTIST SCHOOL

As bad as it was for Teresa in the government-run grammar school, things were about to get worse. As soon as she hit high school, her father was transferred to be a mission preacher at another pueblo sixty miles away. Teresa now left behind her reservation friends forever, no longer even allowed the minimal contact of overhearing their chatter at school about kiva ceremonies and sweat lodges. In her missionary-taught high school, she was given serious training in the Christian fundamentalist ways. Along with the handful of other teenagers in her class, she was given the abhorrent job of proselytizing to incarcerated people at the county jail. Throughout high school, Teresa continued to hide in closets when donors to the reservation missionary program came to visit her family at home or church. But the thought that she was being trained to become "one of them" was what frightened her most.

A WAY OUT

Teresa needn't have worried about becoming one of them.

When Teresa and her sister were offered the opportunity to attend a Baptist college in Texas, her parents—buying into the importance of middle class education—seized on it as good fortune: a "way out" of the poverty of the reservation. The teenaged Teresa was on track to becoming the first in her community to get a college education. Teresa had only a vague notion of what this meant. She received a brochure with photos of white, middle class, laughing co-eds, their blond hair swept into short bobs and pony tails. They seemed to whisper from the pages: *join us and you will have it all*. All she knew was that somehow Christian fundamentalism had become woven into the notion of expanded economic and social opportunities: the promised land of salvation entered through the twin doors of higher education and Jesus Christ. Deep in Teresa's heart, however, the teenager suspected that her parents' notion of a "way out" was, in truth, a path that was destined to take her further and further away from her authentic self, not to mention everything she cared about.

In fact, while the path she was put on did succeed in moving her away from her traditional reservation culture and community, her conflict about becoming "one of them" turned out to be unfounded. For the remainder of her years in Baptist college, Teresa was an outsider. Worse, Teresa recalled, weeping once again, she was in a kind of no man's land of betwixt and between—no longer part of her reservation's life or culture but not embraced by her fellow students, either. She was, in her own bitter words, a "misfit."

AN OUTSIDER

The amount of the scholarship that Teresa had been offered was $250 a semester, which was to include books and tuition. Her parents were delighted, not realizing that the sum would not be enough to cover such basics as food, clothing and toiletries. Before she left, Teresa picked through the charitable hand-me-downs, trying to find an outfit that would come closest to matching the outfits she'd seen in the college brochure. Thinking herself presentable, she accepted a charitable ride from a church member to

Texas and disembarked on her new life. The heat of Texas was about the only thing that greeted her warmly. Teresa realized, looking at the gathering co-eds in front of her dormitory, that the girls were dressed in sandals and summery dresses. She had never heard of such a thing: clothing that changed with the seasons. Who could afford such a luxury? "I would just sit in class and look at those people, overwhelmed by the variety of their outfits, which seemed to change daily."

And then, too, even if she could have afforded the right clothes, in the Texas of the 1960s, there was what Teresa refers to as "that whole civil rights thing." Teresa and her sister had the darkest skins in the school. The school was proud of its Indian students, using her to prove the lengths of Christian charity. "I could never truly fit in," she said.

The first semester Teresa was at college was particularly painful. "I didn't know how to study. My parents didn't get past the tenth grade. They valued education, but didn't have one themselves. Somehow I'd made it through high school without studying. But college was a whole other thing."

PROBATION

By the end of her first semester, Teresa had been put on academic probation, forced to go before the Dean of Academics. Aware of the eyes that were upon his Indians, he gave her "one more semester." She replied: "I'll try to do better." This was a ritual that was to repeat itself semester after semester. In truth, the last thing Teresa wanted was to be given another chance. But she was so unschooled in the ways of academia; she didn't even know she could quit.

The pressures of social discomfort, financial strain and academic pressure bubbled to a head early on. Teresa had been given a job working in the cafeteria, passing out food to students. "I didn't even know how to use utensils properly. Nobody had ever shown me the basics of social etiquette." Trying to live on the $250 per semester, the girls were too poor to buy meal tickets. "My sister depended on me to take scraps of leftovers back to the dormitory for her. As it turns out, someone on the kitchen staff spied on me, gathering evidence. The day came that I put a discarded muffin in my pocket and the supervisor cornered me: 'You're stealing food.' When I explained the circumstances, not only did they admonish me for what they called stealing, but they told me that I had sinned. They called the pastor from the church that I was attending, who came with his wife to the dormitory. I knew my dorm-mates were listening in and this thing about the food: it was such a big deal. The pastor basically listened to my story and then responded: a sin is a sin is a sin."

Teresa couldn't believe what was happening. She knew, in her heart, that what she had done was compassionate caring: a moral act taking priority over the injunction against stealing, in keeping with the reciprocal values of her traditional upbringing. Nevertheless, she felt humiliated by the incident: a sense of burning shame that still sends pink into her cheeks in the retelling.

Dredging up whatever bit of pride she had left, she refused to return to the kitchen, leaving the girls without food. Hearing of her plight, one of Teresa's professors tried to help out by offering her a job working for his wife. While Teresa was grateful for the money, the experience did nothing to reduce her sense of being a total misfit. "I went there to be her house cleaner. I'd do whatever she told me to do: mop the floors, do the dusting. I thought I could do anything she asked—and be happy to do it. Then one day, she asked me to paint her nails. To somebody else, this may not have been a big deal. But I had no idea where to start. My family's whole existence had always centered on working with our hands. We chopped wood, kneaded bread, fed the animals. Our fingernails were unadorned and painting nails was neither in our culture nor in our tradition. When I told her I didn't know how, I'd expected her to be angry. What I got was worse: pity."

BOLTING

Teresa couldn't wait to leave—thinking that by leaving her fundamentalist college and community behind she would at last be free of shame. Regretting that it had taken her so long to figure out how to drop out of school, she eventually took the first step on the long road towards the retrieval of her pride—and an advanced degree. Having learned the ropes, she enrolled at the University of

New Mexico where she completed her undergraduate education. The moment she left Texas, she dropped her affiliation with the church and began to build a life for herself outside of fundamentalism. Like many of the women interviewed for the study, Teresa underestimated how much it would take to reclaim an authentic life. Her exit strategy, in a refrain that echoes my own frantic bolt to freedom, centered on marriage to a white student she met while attending school. "Talk about leaping from the frying pan into the fire! My husband was training to be an engineer—as exacting and rigid as the culture I had hoped to escape. I realize now that I had become socialized to emotional abuse—first my father, then the church and now my husband."

EXPOSURE

The more successful her husband became, the quieter he got. "I could feel him judging me all the time. Distressed, I began gaining weight. He would take me out to restaurants but I could tell that he was ashamed of me. It got so that I couldn't eat in front of him. I would just sit there with my head hanging down, my plate untouched." Then one day, she came home to the news that he was leaving her for another woman.

"I can see, in retrospect, that was the best thing that could have happened to me. Instead of feeling ashamed, for once, I got angry! I vowed then and there that I would never let myself feel shame again." Hot on this vow's heels, Teresa felt another unexpected emotion: longing. She missed her tribe—her connection to her original community. "Connecting to your people, it's like feeding yourself." She didn't know how she was ever going to go home again, but she knew that the rest of her life was to be about trying.

"It's always a battle reclaiming your self...it slips away and you have to go running after it." Before Teresa could return home, she had unfinished business to do. In the state school system, the much-pitied Indian who had spent most of her early college years on scholastic probation, went back for a Master's degree in health education and a Ph.D. in sociology. "Now people always say 'you are so ambitious.' I am ambitious—but not in the way they think. The only thing that motivates me is working hard to be myself."

AN AUTHENTIC LIFE

The sun had set long ago. Earlier on in the day, there had been numerous interruptions. Teresa's nephew had come in bearing a Christmas gift for his favorite aunt. She had one for him in return. They had sung a Christmas carol for their visitor, then, upon Teresa's request, a traditional Indian song. Her sister had stopped by to borrow some Ajax. Then her mother called. The washing machine had broken. We had driven the mile through the reservation to wait with her for the repairman to arrive. Through it all, we had talked. Now, back in Teresa's adobe home, we were so engrossed in the conversation, we hadn't even gotten up to turn on the lights. In a quiet but steady voice, Teresa told me about her decision to move back to the reservation, a gutsy move since many of the old-timers still think of her and her family as "those bortes."

"You get to a point in your life when you do what's right for you because it's in your heart—not what other people have planned for you. It's wonderful to walk outside at midnight and not feel any sort of fear of the dark. I have nothing to be afraid of now—except, maybe, my own tendency to slip back."

In the past 35 years, Teresa has only been to church a couple of times and then, only because her mother begged her to take her. Teresa has returned to what she calls "my Indian ways."

"I feel at home because there's something about expressing yourself in an Indian way that is very intimate. Nobody has to tell you to be kind. Nobody has to tell you to reciprocate. Nobody has to tell you to take the Breath of the trees, of the clouds. If you feel like you have to throw the corn meal out before you go to greet the sun to show you are a good woman, that is your business. It's very private! My moral code is to walk with dignity and to allow dignity to others."

RECLAIMING ASPECTS OF CHRISTIANITY

When Teresa's father died, she gave him a traditional Indian burial while other family members gave him a fundamentalist Christian memorial. Teresa refused to attend. With his death, attendance at her father's church diminished. Teresa had heard that the missionaries had retired "somewhere out west." She still struggles with her family members who are now split in two: half following the traditional Indian ways, half still bound to fundamentalism.

She looks for bridges whenever possible, recognizing that there are certain aspects of Christianity with which she still resonates. "The Golden Rule meshes with our tribal code. And in the end, Christian fundamentalism did lead me to pursue an education. Now that I am educated, I can see aspects of Jesus' teaching that are consistent with our principle of reciprocity, even if I didn't experience them myself."

But it was her departure from Christian fundamentalism that gave her the gift she now values the most: freedom of choice. While she never remarried and has no children, she takes comfort in her extended family and relationship to her community, marginal though she might be.

"It's slow and I am still inhibited: but I have worked hard to reclaim my voice—a voice that counts. What I know is this: Life is right now. Rushing off to go fix my mother's washing machine is what life is about. Now, I choose to be earthward not upward. I choose to acknowledge all things feminine. If I want to get up and go out and feed the dogs, I want to feel free to do that. I want to give with dignity. If my nephew drops by, I want to give him the dignity of the moment. And if my sister drops by to borrow some Ajax, I want to say 'take the whole thing: the whole can.' Dignity as the antidote to shame: it's everything to me."

Talk about shame! It wasn't just the heat off the potbelly stove that brought a flush to my own face. How could I, Jimmy Smull, ever have been taught to interpret the Great Commission as an excuse to culturally dominate other people? With every bundle of clothes I packed off to reservations like Teresa's—in the name of Christian charity—I unthinkingly had delivered the insidious message that "Our people are superior to yours; our religion is superior to yours." In the name of Jesus' love, we condemned this woman's sacred Indian beliefs, alienated her from her community and sent her forth to become an outcast in the predominantly white, discriminating Christian fundamentalist community where she was sent to college. She no longer fit anywhere.

While Teresa paid a much higher price for her education than had I, we both found freedom from fundamentalism through our academic pursuits. As women, we had both suffered from a theology and culture that privileged the male over the female. Perhaps it is no accident that both Teresa and I pursued academic paths that led us to careers that, especially at the time, were dominated by men. For me, the fields were real estate and anthropology. For Teresa, it was sociology. Imagine how much courage it took for Teresa to negotiate the path from a shamed outsider, perennially condemned to the academic probation list, to a well-respected professor standing before a classroom of students, including blond co-eds and white boys in trendy, seasonally appropriate clothes? Even more daunting for both of us had been the task of re-visioning ourselves as "authorities." At the Mind, Body, Spirit conference I sponsored in New York, one of the attendees stood up and asked how she could get over her sense of inferiority around authority figures? Author and Reverend Karen Boland replied that each authority figure is just a person who happens to know a little bit more about one subject than others. At the same time, the participant, too, knows more about certain subjects than do others. Karen told her not to be intimidated by the "uniform", be it a doctor's smock, an attorney's expensive suit, or—in the case of women breaking from fundamentalism—a minister's robes.

I thought back to my first meeting with Teresa. We had both been covered head to toe with the fine red dust of mother earth. There were no facades to hide behind—the uniforms had been shed along with our Christian fundamentalist beliefs. Now we were on new terrain: pioneering a life beyond the bonds of shame. Teresa already had her doctorate and I was on the way to getting mine. We had both come a long way since our days of suffering silently in Baptist schools and colleges, our authentic selves hidden beneath layers of toxic beliefs. My graduate education had taught me to dig deep as an anthropologist, into the hard ground of prehistoric sites, looking for clues from the past. Having met Teresa, I now knew that others—including some I would never have expected—had also embarked on the project of our lives, reclaiming precious treasures of the past and future from the depths of our souls.

CHAPTER TEN

Carmen: Healing Fear

Fear
The feeling that evil or danger is near; dread.
The World Book Dictionary, 17th Edition

My conversation with Teresa stayed with me throughout the remainder of my research project—and now through the writing of this book. Shame is such a destructive emotion—particularly when it is inflicted in the name of religion. Despite the recovery of her authentic self—the reclamation of a life of meaning—Teresa was still visibly upset when forced to recall the emotional abuse of missionaries who saw their commission to deliver God's "great love" to the impoverished Indians they so pitied. When it came to fear, however, Teresa had come to recognize that the greatest threat to her well being was her own persistent tendency to buy into their toxic point of view about herself, her people and her beliefs.

Teresa feared the missionaries and her own feelings of shame. Horrible as these fears are, she had saved herself from the greatest dread of all: the fear of God. Unlike most other co-researchers, including myself, Teresa never bought into the notion of heaven and hell: the tortured version of a God who resorts to threats of vengeful anger, sometimes with apparently little provocation. Carmen was not so fortunate.

I had known Carmen casually for several years as the sweet young woman who worked at the gift and flower shop in my neighborhood shopping center. I felt that I had watched her blossom. From visit to visit, she progressed from dating to engagement to marriage to pregnancy to young motherhood. But on this particular visit, all signs of radiance were absent.

"Is something the matter?" I inquired, as Carmen gift-wrapped a little gift box I'd chosen as a birthday present for my daughter-in-law.

"My husband's been transferred to Florida," she replied. Carmen explained that she was born and raised in Florida—and it wasn't by mere accident that she had taken up residence in California, as far away across the country as she could go. Now, with the impending move back to Florida, she was being forced to confront the shadows of her past. As she put the finishing touches on the gift box, she whispered across the counter: "Do you know anything about Christian fundamentalism?"

Boy, did we have a lot to talk about! We couldn't coordinate our schedules before her move, so it was that several months later, Carmen was picking me up at the airport in Miami for the next in my series of research interviews. Carmen was dressed casually— jeans, a t-shirt and sandals. She wore her dark brown hair long, tucked back behind an ear with two tasteful piercings. In the back seat of her aging Toyota was Kirk, her nine-month old little boy. We drove to her home on the outskirts of Miami, a bedroom community for young couples with families. Carmen obviously doted on her son. Our long day's conversation was woven into the pattern of her attentive mothering: changing the baby; feeding the baby, pausing to include Kirk's high-pitched chattering into the dialogue and—blessedly—occasionally putting the baby down for his nap. When the phone rang from time to time, it was Carmen's husband. A pilot for a private company, he checked in on Carmen and the baby several times both in the air and on the ground: the picture of domestic tranquility.

THE BIRTH OF FUNDAMENTALISM

The return to Florida had, as Carmen predicted, unearthed some old fears and concerns. But happily, her years of hard emotional work reclaiming her authentic self from Christian fundamentalism were holding up better than expected. Nowhere was the distance Carmen had traveled more obvious than in the contrast between the lively warmth of her home and, as she described it, the rigid environment in which she'd been raised. While Kirk pushed every button on his airplane-shaped plastic toddler seat, complete with a beeping, honking electronic dashboard, Carmen began her story.

Carmen's mother was still a teenager when she'd married her

Navy husband, a young sailor with a quick and violent temper. She was only 18 years old when Carmen was born, the baby's birth adding tension to an already borderline situation. Carmen's earliest memory is running down the street with her mother, with only the clothes on their backs, her father screaming after them never to return. Carmen now knows that her mother, pregnant at the time with Carmen's younger brother, had just been violently kicked in the stomach and that Carmen, herself, had narrowly escaped her father's blows. In fact, the kick to her mid-section had put Carmen's mother into early labor. At the difficult delivery, her father was nowhere to be found. But a friend of her mother, Andrew, also in the military, sat by her side and helped her through the ordeal. They were married as soon as her mother's uncontested divorce was finalized, a few months later. Carmen was only one and one-half years old when not only Andrew but also Andrew's religion—Christian fundamentalism—came into her life.

Carmen has no memory of her stepfather ever attending church or even reading the Bible. But Andrew had a firm grip, nevertheless, on the rigid rules of conduct that he resolutely equated to a God-fearing life. Passing it down the line the way he'd been taught, Andrew's interpretation of Godly behavior included the understanding that children were to be neither seen nor heard. Emotionally removed, Andrew ate alone in the living room while the rest of the family took their meals at the dining room table. "He zoned out and didn't hear a word we were saying." When Andrew wasn't at work, he was otherwise occupied with extreme, addictive behavior: consumed with uninterrupted bouts of watching television, working at the computer at ten hours a stretch and non-stop smoking.

Andrew convinced his young wife that the children needed to attend church every week, even if they—the parents—did not. From the time Carmen was three years old, the church bus would arrive every Wednesday afternoon and Sunday morning, and the children—Carmen, her brother and her two stepbrothers—would be transported to religious school, social gatherings and services. Carmen remembers sharing a microphone onboard with the bus driver's daughter, singing hymns karaoke-style, like "The Old

Rugged Cross."

On a hill faraway stood an old rugged cross,
the emblem of suffering and shame:

And I love that old cross, where the dearest and best
for a world of lost sinners was slain.

Carmen took to church. In fact, rather than any particular games or toys as favorite childhood memories, Carmen remembers that praying was her greatest satisfaction. "I could be having the most horrible day of my life, but when I prayed, I felt good. Praying was probably my greatest satisfaction, knowing that somebody listened and somebody cared. Somebody heard what I was saying."

Church was such a refuge for the little Carmen, she remembers dreading Mondays and Tuesdays as "days of the week I couldn't go to church, even if I wanted to." At the age of four, Carmen asked to be baptized. The church required a conversation between the child and the minister to demonstrate Carmen's understanding of church fundamentals. The four-year-old Carmen memorized the booklet, "The Plan of Salvation" and convinced the minister that she understood that because of her sinfulness, God's son, Jesus Christ, had come to this earth and died for our sins. Carmen assured the minister that she had repented her sins. At the age of four, Carmen trusted that her acceptance of Jesus Christ as her Savior was the only way she would get to go to heaven.

"The minister had never baptized someone so young. When I answered his questions perfectly, he relented and set a date. I urgently wanted to be saved!"

Carmen recalls her baptismal transformation into a "soldier for Christ." Eventually, her Sunday school teachers and older student leaders entrusted her with the key to the classroom, gave her the job of putting out the hymn books, assigned her to take up the students' offerings and bring them to the church office along with many other special tasks. She even remembers taking pride in turning in friends who had broken one or another of the church rules. "I felt like I was in an inner circle."

When Carmen invited girls over for sleepovers, she made sure that the children spent the night reading the Bible and talking about God. By the time she hit her pre-teen years, Carmen had read the Bible front to back six times—"chapters and chapters" every night. When she reached the end, she would start right over from the beginning. The sleepovers were but one of the tools in her proselytizing arsenal. "I couldn't accept invitations to friends' homes or churches because I had been taught that only my church knew the real God. Instead, I tried my hardest to get my friends to go to church with me. I felt like I had to have a new person every week to introduce as a visitor. Everyone was depending on me. If I didn't, I was concerned that something bad was going to happen." Carmen won much praise from the church for her exemplary behavior. In truth, however, beneath the privileged exterior ran a current of fear.

"While I invested a lot in feeling like I was an insider—one of the family—in retrospect, I realize that I never felt quite as secure as the actual children of the minister and heads of the church. They were the real insiders and they had a certain amount of power over the rest of us. I was only an insider as long as I had their approval, so whatever they told me to do, I did it. To me, disobeying them bore a huge price: if I lost their approval, I would be doomed to an eternity in hell."

GREAT-GRANDMA'S TONGUES

Carmen can't pin down the moment her happiness over the salvation of heaven turned into perfectionism fueled by fear of going to hell, but she does know when her undercurrent of fear first burst forth in a lava of raw terror. With the baby Kirk snoozing momentarily in her arms, Carmen whispered that her passion for Jesus did not go unnoticed. Her stepfather's grandmother chose Carmen to accompany her to various tent meetings and revivals held throughout the South: a great family honor. But for Carmen, this was a nightmare just about to begin. Her great-grandmother practiced a special form of fundamentalism: Pentecostal Christianity. In the Pentecostal revivals, charismatic ministers stirred emotions to a fever pitch. Congregants threw themselves at the altar and writhed on the ground before the cross. Carmen, not even out of single digits, was submitted to the chaotic, hysterical church services, where in the name of worshipping God, people acted out all kinds of behavior. Some yelled out phrases as if ventriloquists were controlling them, others jumped around, falling down, and moaning until they had become exhausted. At age seven, Carmen watched her great-grandmother get swept up in the frenzy of a Reverend Jimmy Swaggart revival, screaming out the seemingly never-ending stream of unintelligible syllables Pentecostals call "speaking in tongues." For believers, the words and sounds came straight from the Holy Spirit and could be interpreted by other believers as carrying sacred meaning. Watching her great-grandmother screaming nonsense syllables while banging her fist down repeatedly on the chair before her, Carmen had a very different interpretation. She feared that great-grandma had become possessed by demons!

"I started crying, running to strangers to protect me from my own great-grandmother. I didn't want to talk to her—let alone go home with her—because I was so afraid that somehow the devil would get me, too." At her stepfather's insistence and mother's compliance, the trips with great-grandma continued, however. Another time, Carmen remembers being taken to a church where everybody was in a kind of trance, staring off into space with vacant eyes.

For Carmen, fear became a way of life. Not only was she afraid of going to the revivals and their terrifying transformation of her great-grandmother into a wild woman, but before long, she was equally scared of staying away.

"In the face of pressure from my family, I had been convinced that going with great-grandma to revivals—not to mention continuing to do whatever I needed to stay connected to the inner circle in my own church—was my only hope of avoiding hell. Talk about being afraid! Great-grandma used to tell me that if I were to do something as little as cutting my fingernails on a Sunday, I was going to hell. We couldn't cut anything on Sunday—not even a loaf of bread. She would tell me if I wanted to wear earrings, I was going to hell. She was so strict, my brothers and I couldn't play cards on the kitchen table because that would mean we were destroying God's holy table. There were so many rules, I couldn't keep them straight and I dreaded inadvertently making a mistake and ending up paying for it forever."

At some point early on, Carmen started praying for forgiveness every night whether she could think of a particular sin she had committed or not. No longer did she take refuge in prayers of comfort, such as "Fear thou not; for I am with thee" (Isaiah 41:10). Instead, she read herself to sleep with passages she heard at the revivals, such as:

> *The Son of man shall send forth his angels, and they shall gather out of his kingdom all things that offend, and them which do iniquity; And shall cast them into a furnace of fire; there shall be wailing and gnashing of teeth.*
> MATTHEW (13: 41–42)

Of all of the participants in my research study, Carmen mentioned the word "fear" the most: 33 times. She used the expression "scared to death" an additional four. "I was scared to death to do anything because I thought I would go to hell."

As Carmen whispered her feelings of being overwhelmed and alienated, my own painful memories stirred awake. While Carmen had originally begged for baptism, I recalled that fearful moment when I wanted to bolt from the baptismal font, out of the church never to return. I felt so alone; my only hope for avoiding an eternity in hell was the cold water before me, threatening to swallow me whole. This was not a euphoric moment, nor did I hear any angels singing. I just felt my heart pounding, reminding myself that this was the price of belonging. The situation was too overwhelming for a little girl my age to have to "prove" my salvation. I was a spectacle on display in front of 3000 hungry eyes.

For children like Carmen and myself, immersed in psychological manipulation at such a young age, release to freedom from fear is something that comes only through struggle. For Carmen, the move from childhood towards adolescence began to breakup the airtight patterns of her rigid and terrifying childhood. Until pre-adolescence,

Carmen's authentic self had been more than hidden—it had been buried beneath the toxic waste of a belief system based on power and fear. Then at ten, she got the news that her stepfather was to be transferred to Okinawa, moving them away from Florida—and from great-grandma's revivals. The second stage of the process of breaking free from Christian fundamentalism was about to begin.

THE REACTIVE SELF

Because Carmen's stepfather was in the Air Force, Carmen, her brother and stepbrothers all attended secular schools located on the military base. In Okinawa, Carmen relished exposure to children of many races, nationalities and religions. Far from Florida, she had the opportunity to befriend Mormons and Buddhists studying them for signs of damnation. She could not find any. Like me, she just could not buy the family line that so many of her friends were all going to hell no matter how good they were. "If God is so almighty and so loving, why would he send good people to a fiery pit? Why would somebody, just because he believed something different, go to hell? How can they say that Jesus is right but Buddha is wrong? I wanted proof."

Exposed to the scientific method in junior high, Carmen started asking questions. She asked her Sunday school teacher, "How do you know that Jesus is real?" The answer: "Well, we just have to believe." She asked her mother: "If we have souls, what happens if we step on an ant? That's a living thing, so it has a soul, too." Her mother resounded: "It's just not the same."

"How was I going to believe that anything about Christian fundamentalism is true if they couldn't prove to me that this stuff happened?"

At 14, her father was transferred again, this time to California. By now, Carmen was studying evolution in science class, her probing questions falling on reasonable responses.

"One of my teachers introduced me to historical approaches to the Bible. It was so obvious to me that the Bible was written by human beings with agendas. While they may have been well-meaning people, they obviously made mistakes. And, while we're at it, who says they didn't lie about things? All humans lie, why not the authors of the Bible? When I read about the King James revision of the Bible—proof that humans had a hand in the Bible I read cover to cover six times as the infallible word of God—it hit me like a ton of bricks! I'd been brainwashed!"

The baby's cries alerted us that he had woken from his nap. Positioned strategically at Carmen's side, I was busy handing her lotions and powders as she changed Kirk's diaper. Our conversation continued uninterrupted, but at a higher pitch, as the tape recorder captured not only the animation of our mutual discovery, but the increasingly delighted gurgles of the child.

I completely related to Carmen's persistent questioning of the Absolute Truth of the Bible. As Carmen and I compared notes we realized that we had both been told to rely on the Bible as God's unquestionable authority. This was the fallback position of our teachers and parents. They responded to any of our inquiries, no matter how well reasoned, researched or thought-through, with the admonition "to have faith." Carmen laughed out loud remembering that when she was young, she had been so desperate at one point to talk to someone "outside the system"—somebody other than her parents or Sunday school teachers—that she had seized on the church bus driver who drove her and her brothers to church. "I was sure he would tell me the truth. When he also told me to have faith and not ask questions—but to believe in the truth of what I was being taught—I realized they were all in on it."

At 14, Carmen was already deeply questioning her faith. Then in 1987, the newspaper headlines and airwaves blared the news that her great-grandmother's hero, Reverend Jimmy Swaggart, had been found in a motel room with a prostitute. This controversy came on the heels of the fall of another minister and televangelist, Jim Bakker who had become entangled with Jessica Hahn. Swaggart was given a two-year disciplinary action, restricted from preaching for the duration by the Louisiana District of the Assemblies of God.

"One night, I lay there in bed, turning over and over again, thinking about everything I had ever been told. The next morning, I stopped going to church. Just like that. I never went again." For a while, she got phone calls from the church asking her to return, but she kept making up excuses. The most difficult confrontation was when she sat her mother down and told her "I don't believe in hell anymore." Her mother's response: "I've failed you."

After yet another scandal involving a woman, Swaggart returned to televangelism, explaining that "Jesus had paid the price" for Swaggart's sins. Carmen doesn't buy it.

"It had nothing to do with Jesus. In fact, I think everything in the church was invented to scare people into doing whatever the people in power wanted them to do. I think that was created a long time ago, and it has been carried along from generation to generation."

Recalling the emphasis on proselytizing that had comprised the core of her Sunday school education, she spoke of the church as a "numbers game." How many members can they get, how much money can they raise? After the falls of Bakker and Swaggart, Carmen also believes that theft and embezzlement run rampant in the church. "I don't trust anyone who has power in the church: ministers or authority figures of any kind. In fact, I always turn off the televangelists, sensing evil behind their manipulations."

I'd had this conversation before, with my husband. As a child, he grew up in a family who thought of themselves as Protestant, but never attended church. Even though he has no memory of his family ever talking about religion, he does remember having been given a tiny Bible as a child. Because he had received the Bible during World War II, Les had tucked a little American flag inside the front cover, and remembers praying for the safe return of the soldiers from the battlefield.

He went to college, studying economics. His sophomore year, he decided to attend a Methodist church in Los Angeles "to see what religion was all about." The church was in a wealthy area. There were rows and rows of well-dressed people and their beautiful cars, lined up for them outside after services in the church parking lot. Looking back, my husband remembers going about half a dozen times. He listened carefully to the sermons, followed the prayers and rituals, but failed to find the logic in them. Nevertheless, the minister thought of him as something of a catch, inviting him to get more involved with the church. But he decided that if he really wanted to understand what makes religion tick, he was not going to find it in a pew. Instead, he enrolled in an elective at college called

"The Psychology of Religion." There, whatever fascination he had with religion came to a skidding halt. Auditing the class was a group of Baptist ministers. They, alongside the enrolled students, listened intently as the teacher explained the manipulative use of ritual, guilt and unworthiness as tools of church membership, development, maintenance and control. While my husband and the other students were trying to get a grip on religion as a sociological phenomenon, the ministers were quietly taking notes, looking for ways to use psychology as a more efficient means of controlling their members. He was appalled!

Having grown up outside organized religion, my husband had been able to use his logic and critical thinking skills to unlock the secrets behind the power and monetary manipulations of many church leaders. For someone like Carmen—and myself, for that matter—the ability to shake off a lifetime of brainwashing may require years of diligent work on multiple levels. In addition to her own curiosity and observations, what inadvertently saved Carmen from total immersion in fear was her stepfather's multiple moves, her separation from her home church and entanglements—and her exposure to outside influences. Carmen had been able to begin healing her reactive self and to enter the final of the three-stages: the reclamation of her wisdom.

RECLAMATION

Carmen was barely out of her teen-aged years when we first met at the gift shop in my neighborhood. Some years later, as I watched the young mother alternately coddle, feed and engage her child, I felt deeply moved to compliment her on how much she had accomplished. "You have no idea," she responded. As the daylight started to fade, Carmen set out a simple dinner for us and continued her story.

"There were so many rules about who to date, and what not to do with a boy when I did go out with him socially, I basically bagged the whole dating thing until I'd left the church." Once she'd determined that church was over for her, Carmen gave herself permission to look outside the church community for prospects. When she met her husband, she knew "instantly" that he was somebody she'd like to get to know better. The invitation was returned. Only as their relationship deepened did Carmen realize that her escape from Christian fundamentalism was not complete. In fact, Carmen now understands, the reclamation of her authentic self may well be the job of a lifetime.

As Carmen tells it, one moonlit night, her future husband admitted to her some adolescent indiscretions that probably would have passed with a wink and a finger-wag in the "normal" world. But in the world of Carmen's upbringing, the unredeemed "sins" would have been seen as no less than a one-way ticket to hell. Could she forgive him? If she did forgive him, was he nevertheless doomed? Love and commonsense prevailed and the two married. Carmen is now at peace with her husband's past, having cast her vote with the compassionate rather than vengeful God. But the two concepts of God continue to wrestle, popping up in surprising ways and places.

One of the places the dueling Gods showed up was under her bikini line, in the form of a hidden tattoo. She kept the tattoo a secret from her mother and father for two years, afraid to tell them about her body art. "I know that my father would think of it as a defilement and I just don't want to have to deal with any of his stuff about burning in hell over it. I know now that having a tattoo doesn't change my destiny: and in any case, I want nothing to do with a God who would punish me so harshly for such a little thing."

A bigger issue unfortunately not as easy to hide is the tension between Carmen and her mother over how Kirk is being raised. "She wants me to do with my son what was done to me. Here I am, still struggling with guilt over having dragged so many of my friends into that church, and my mother wants me to do that to my own son? To tell you the truth, I sincerely hope that everybody I witnessed to has gotten free of Christian fundamentalism, particularly if I played a role starting them down the path to conversion."

Ironically, Carmen's move to Florida in support of her husband's career had put her but a stone's throw from her parent's home. The week before I arrived, Carmen and her mother had gotten into an upsetting interrogation concerning why Carmen had turned her back on her religious upbringing. Carmen had to walk out of her mother's house in order to avoid a full-out fight. While Carmen's mother had volunteered to take the baby while Carmen worked, Carmen had subsequently made the difficult decision to look for someone else to keep her son during the day. "I profoundly disagree with my parents on some key issues. I know now that it's enough to teach my baby to be a good person. Kirk could come home someday with 15 earrings in his eyebrow: as long as he doesn't do anything illegal and treats others with respect."

Carmen cherished her freedom from toxic religion — but it came with a high price. In fact, knowing that some of the gifts I'd purchased at her shop had been for my own mother, now deceased, Carmen asked me for advice.

"How did you bridge the gap between honoring your father and your mother while holding on to your authentic self?" she asked. I told her that it had been a slow process because I loved my parents deeply, but increasingly had come to realize over the years that I could not honor the absolute truths they represent. I told Carmen about a time I had taken my mother to an anthropology museum, pointing out to her actual skulls and recreated busts of Neanderthal and Cro-Magnon man, explaining to her that these were among the earliest human beings: our ancestors. When my mother took in the prehistoric skulls, she muttered vehemently at them: "You're not my relatives!" Mother finally got used to the idea that I was going to continue my academic interest in archeology, exposed to the most prominent archaeologists and paleontologists in the field. But mother had one request: that I "witness" to them. "Scientists are atheists, you know!" she implored me. Just as I had come a long, long way from my parents' heartfelt belief in Creationism, I understood how far Carmen had come in asserting her own divergent truth from her parents — especially when, in their eyes she was dooming herself to an eternity in hell by doing so.

Just how had I negotiated the treacherous path that led me from the bosom of my family's religion to the freedom of my authentic self? While the dominant emotion for Carmen had been fear, for me, it had been resentment. For many years, I resented the fact that my parents made a decision on my behalf to make a radical change in our family's life over which I had no control. I could not understand how they could relinquish confidence in their own judgment in deference to an outside source who claimed to know a better Truth, burying not only their authentic selves beneath layers of toxicity, but taking me along with them. I could have let the emotion consume me, but for the gift of a realization I'd had not long ago. From my position as an adult, it began to dawn on me that I had birthed and nurtured my resentment against my parents solely from the point of view of a child. Over time, I came increasingly to understand that all adults refrain from sharing certain aspects of their lives with their children—often for good, loving reasons. The truth is, I had quite simply not been privy to all of the circumstances that led my mother and my father to walk down that church aisle to ask forgiveness for their sins that fateful day when I was only nine years old. If I did not have the whole story, how could I, the scientist, gather the proof I needed to justify holding a grudge against them?

But what was the alternative? Simply this. I could be true to my authentic self: a spirit that had more often than not found the way to be gracious and loving rather than self-righteous. I could be compassionate in place of judgmental. Of course there would be times when my parents and I would disagree. I had to decide which were the critical occasions to which I must arise—and which were not central to my identity. In time, I learned to let many opportunities for confrontation pass when I was in their presence. This was not the way I wished things had to be, but as I've learned to free myself from the rigidity of black and white thinking, I've also had to find ways to appreciate spending more time in the gray areas of less than perfect solutions. By learning to draw boundaries and protect my authentic self, I could be more generous to my parents. The ultimate test of my compassion came when my father and then my mother died, leaving it in my hands to give them Christian fundamentalist funerals. Even though I would not go to church for myself, I honored their wishes, providing a tribute to their lives with their favorite hymns and Bible verses. I could do this only by actively remembering that while I was raised by them, I am not them. I was not their empty slate, my authentic self rewritten according to their programmed script. I had poetry of my own that could not be denied.

It was getting late and soon it would be time for Carmen to take me to the airport. As she readied Kirk for the ride, she said: "It's clear that I do need to draw the line with my parents." Then sighing deeply: "But maybe I can try drawing the line out of compassion for myself and my baby rather than out of fear of them or their religious beliefs. It's worth a try."

It's so hard for people like Carmen and me who were raised with black and white thinking to learn how to live in the grays. I remembered the poem I'd written on a writing retreat while pursuing my doctorate. The poem—the first I'd ever written in my life—put this part of our lives into perspective. One part of the poem reads:

> *Life must honor its roots from which it grows*
> *Just as a tree has a root system that only it knows...*
> *The tree in full bloom for all to gaze*
> *Knows that it all comes together in mysterious ways.*

CHAPTER ELEVEN
Adrian: Healing Anger

Adrian appeared to me as a woman in the prime of her
success. At fifty something, she had just enough extra
weight on her to command attention. Her style was as
blunt and direct as her hair-do: cropped short with the unapologetic
first hints of a peppery gray peeking through thick black strands,
the only obvious reminder of her Armenian ancestry. Despite a
hearty greeting, I have to admit that I found Adrian somewhat
intimidating at first. She had obviously made a success of herself in
her career, firmly shaking my hand in a practiced clasp. I inwardly
found myself wondering what this apparently self-possessed woman
could possibly have in common with those of us, like Teresa and
Carmen, who have struggled so hard with issues of self-esteem.

Looks can be deceiving.

As we settled into two comfortable armchairs overlooking the
busy downtown street below, Adrian began her riveting story. She
took a deep breath and characteristically of Adrian, went right to
the heart of the matter.

"The first thing I knew about myself is that I made a big mistake
being born female, and I shouldn't have done that."

Our paths first intersected during the conference for women that
I sponsored in New York City on the subject of healing body, mind
and spirit. While I had not met Adrian at the conference, she had
been one of many women who had vented her anger about their
fundamentalist upbringings during the stormy session on
spirituality. Years later, while researching possible interview
candidates for my dissertation, I came across the evaluation
questionnaire Adrian had filled out at the end of the seminar. An
Armenian immigrant, a self-made success in the heart of America,
she had indicated that she was anxious to continue to do whatever
she could to save other women from what she had experienced
growing up in a fundamentalist home.

Despite the passing time, when I reached her at her office—an advertising agency in Manhattan—it was as if she had been sitting by the phone waiting for my call. Happily, she was due to travel to San Francisco on a business trip in just a few weeks. We made plans to meet at a lovely suite at the Stanford Court Hotel downtown.

Before Adrian could pause to take a second breath, we were off and running. Any hint of discomfort was eclipsed by the passion and pain of her tale. Adrian was born in Jerusalem into a family fully immersed in Nazarene Christianity. She was the first born in what turned out to be, despite her father's openly stated desire for sons, a family of girls.

THE BAD, BAD APPLE

"It wasn't just my father. It was the whole culture that privileged men over women. Think about it! Jesus had no women disciples. The first time you hear about a woman in the Bible, it's Eve: the bad, bad apple. Yes, there were a few bright lights scattered in the pages: there was Esther, who had nerve. And Mary and Miriam who did this and that. But you know as well as I—they are like apostrophes in the story. Over and over again, the Bible teaches us that it's the woman's job to serve—period. There I was, saying to myself at the age of four or five: 'This can't be true! I can't really be evil just because I'm a girl. I can't really only be born to serve others.' But this is how you feel: getting angry that you can't get outside of it, past it. It's as if your cells have been poisoned. If you are born into this world inferior and sinful, where do you go from there?"

One obvious person to whom she could have turned would have been her mother. To outsiders, it appeared that it was her father who called the shots, not only as the head of the family but as the head of the church as well. The reality was something else.

"Even at four, I knew the truth: mother, deprived of her own voice, had carved out a manipulative role for herself as the power behind the throne." Adrian's Dad had been orphaned at a young age. His uncles had abandoned him to grow up virtually on his own. He had no education. Then he met her mother. At the age of 21, his new wife was steeped in a fear-driven Armenian fundamentalism, the religion of her parents. "Mother was imbued with the extremes of right and wrong. There could be no breaching the gap, no middle ground. She was definitive. More so than my father. He allowed himself to be led by her...looked up to her. She had the education, involved parents, and a manipulative agenda." Adrian's father was her mother's tool, learning the literal truth of the Bible from her as she and her powerful family positioned him for church leadership and what Adrian calls "the perks of power." According to Adrian, he became a minister not to please God, but to please her mother. "I know he felt inferior to her and becoming a minister elevated him in her eyes. Even so, our whole family acted out the charade of the father being the head of the family."

THE PSYCHOLOGY OF DEPRESSION

"There was so much hypocrisy in my upbringing," Adrian says angrily. "On Sunday, my father could preach the love of God, and on Monday, Dad would be emotionally abusing us, always angry about something we had done wrong." It was easy for Adrian and her two younger sisters to make mistakes. "You had to do exactly as was being prescribed or you were evil. You were told that you were not only evil yourself, but an evil influence on others and you were not wanted in this community anymore. Talk about abandonment issues!! Everything was about what we couldn't do— all the negatives: you couldn't dance, wear shorts, swim, go to the movies, drink, smoke or have premarital sex. It was all the authority stuff: men and authority!"

Mother never intervened. When her father was angry or depressed—which was often—his sermons would be full of hellfire and brimstone. One of his favorites was the expulsion of Adam and Eve from the Garden of Eden.

He was fond of embellishing Genesis: "And the Lord God commanded the man Adam, saying, of every tree of the garden thou mayest freely eat. But of the fruit of the tree of the knowledge of good and evil which is in the midst of the garden, God hath said, Ye shall not eat of it, neither shall ye touch it, lest ye die...The serpent tempted the woman to try the fruit, and she did eat of it. She offered some to Adam, and he ate some also. Eve was wicked because she defied God's order, saying unto the serpent 'we may eat of the fruit of the trees of the garden.' And because of her willful disobedience, woman brought down the curse of death upon us all."

Like Teresa's father, who was the only recovering alcoholic in the congregation—and whose specialty was denouncing the wickedness of those who drank—Adrian's father had no clue that the anger he directed at his followers was really intended for himself. He felt ashamed of his inferior education and the poverty of his background. "The worse he felt about himself, the harsher he would act."

The connection between hellfire preaching and depression are born out by research. As David M. Wulff, citing the research of H. Guntrip, writes in *Psychology of Religion*: "Ministers given to hellfire preaching, are likely depressed persons themselves, who find relief from self-castigation by attacking the sins of others." It was not only Adrian's father who projected his own inner pain on others. In the participant Teresa's case, discussed in a previous chapter, her father also used the ministerial platform to vent his anger citing the family's behavior as his excuse. For instance, if one of the children was even a few minutes late for services, he would give a sermon to the entire congregation about the sinfulness of being late. He would bring in any of the old grudges he had with his family members and turn it into the sin of the day. Eli S. Chesen, M.D. in *Religion May Be Hazardous to Your Health*, refers to this kind of behavior as the parental distortion of a religious belief, re-interpreted for his family for the purpose of manipulation and control. "It may take on a new and destructive meaning in the hands of a parent bent on using it as a means to his own end."

CHILDHOOD SHADOWS

As in Teresa's case, the dark currents that ran beneath Adrian's family's religious practices did not confine themselves to the church walls. Adrian remembers that her parents hung a plaque over her bed that lit up at night. The prayer read:

> *Now I lay me down to sleep*
> *I pray the Lord my soul to keep.*
> *If I should die before I wake*
> *I pray the Lord my soul to take.*

In the absence of comforting bedtime stories, cuddles and reassurances from mom and dad that all would be well, Adrian dreaded the location of the poem, positioned as it was, right over her head. "It was morbid—as if the only thing worth talking to God about was dying. Is that what we were living for? To die right?" Adrian sits bolt upright in her chair, her back rigid with emotion. "I hyperventilated all the time—scared to death that somebody was going to die and it was going to be my fault or that I was going to get caught for something I didn't even know I'd done wrong and would end up in hell. It was constant turmoil—trying to be good enough, clever enough—all the time." For Adrian, hell, however, was less the "burning fire thing" her father promoted, and more "this ultimate cosmic humiliation."

As an example of the stress she was under, Adrian remembered being sent to Girl Scouts. She had been told by the leader, a religiously liberal New Yorker who knew nothing about Adrian's religious beliefs, that terrible things would happen if the American flag ever touched the ground. Adrian dreaded taking her turn carrying the flag in the color guard, for fear of what would happen if she should make a mistake. The level of anxiety Adrian experienced would have been incomprehensible to the leader, who had no idea that Adrian's parents had programmed her behavior by threatening their child with punishment by God. So it was the day that Adrian finally got her turn to carry the flag.

"Well," Adrian continued, "the day finally came and you guessed it. I let the damn flag drop to the ground. I lived in mortal fear for days after that the whole United States would collapse because I had messed up. It seemed possible. After all, the Bible was full of magical elements: the seas could part...and all those loaves and fishes out of thin air and all. In some way, there was some force at work in the world that my good or bad behavior could unleash." For Adrian, the impact of the Bible went far beyond written pages of text. "Living in Jerusalem, it was hard to figure out what was real and what was myth. You know, the 'this is what Jesus did here. This is what Jesus did there.' Story presented as history is laid out everywhere you turn."

Adrian, like many of the subjects in my research study, could not voice her fears or her anger out loud. She had learned at a very young age to bury her healthy desire for parental reassurance that all would be well, knowing that her innocent questions and anxieties would be viewed as disloyal and challenging. When she did venture to voice her concerns, she was met with scornful silence or a violent emotional response. In Adrian's case, her anger went underground, burying her authentic self beneath a layer of depression so pervasive, it was perceived by friends and family to be a natural part of her personality. "Not long ago, I confronted my mother about my childhood depression. She claimed not to have had a clue. 'I thought you were just quiet,' my mother replied."

Adrian's comment about her childhood depression reminded me of a similar comment made by another of my co-researchers, Peggy. While interviewing Peggy, the first mention of childhood depression stopped our conversation on a dime. The tense and talkative mother of two young boys had bolted from the sofa to retrieve a yellowing photograph of herself when she was three years old. "Look at this. There is no happiness in my eyes. I don't have a single photograph that shows me smiling. As she flipped through the album, I could, indeed, see pages and pages of a serious looking child, going through the routines of childhood as if they were some kind of burden. In Peggy's words "I was bridled and harnessed to the church's controlling point of view." Neither Adrian's nor Peggy's mothers had the emotional resources needed to reassure their young daughters that making mistakes were a normal part of childhood and that their powers to do bad—and good—were limited. As a result, the girls had no place to turn. Instead, their anger and distress turned inward—invisible, perhaps, but nevertheless potent.

NEGOTIATING LAYERS

At ten years of age, Adrian moved with her family to America. Instead of her father's dark emotions getting better, they worsened. Her father took up a post preaching at a tiny fundamentalist Armenian Church in central California. "It was not an appropriate church for children because the congregation was composed entirely of old people who wanted to hear Armenian sermons in the old language." Adrian longed to go to her community's more popular and Americanized Armenian Presbyterian Church, where she could have worshipped side by side with friends from school. "My father's ego kept us in his church. It was his ego that kept him from doing the right thing. His pride was on the line, especially given his insecurities." For her father, there were the challenges of integration, shame over his accent and language difficulties, among others.

"My father wouldn't learn English so there was always this language thing going around in our house. He learned to read English but he refused to speak it. We all spoke Armenian at home but mother knew English, even finding work in the community as an English teacher. Looking back, I think my father was insecure about his accent and didn't want to expose himself to ridicule. So here I was with two younger sisters, all of us speaking Armenian in varying degrees of competence: the youngest one could barely speak it at all. We could understand what our father was saying when he spoke to us, but we didn't have the means to fully express ourselves back to him." During her elementary school years, Adrian bared the dysfunction as best she could, but reiterates that she was seriously depressed from the age of four or five.

The psychologist L. Seligman, cited in *Abnormal Psychology*, suggests that childhood depression is the result of "learned helplessness." "The concept...assumes that helplessness is learned in early life experiences in which the child comes to feel that nothing he or she does counts in making life more pleasant or less unpleasant. Given that attitude of hopelessness, the individual subsides into depressive inactivity." Seligman finds parallels between helplessness and depression, proposing that treatment of depression provides "learning experiences that undo the sense of hopelessness about the effect of what one does."

While many children require therapy to transcend the hopelessness, Adrian considers it to have been "dumb luck" that she found salvation at the age of 12—in the local public library.

"I went every day I could after school and sat there and read and read and read," Adrian explains. After the anti-intellectualism of fundamentalist faith, Adrian relished in the irreverence of authors, scientists and scholars who dared to question "everything." Just as important, however, was the discovery that she could get away with finding a place outside of her home and church where she could be by herself. "They didn't know what the hell I was reading." At 17, she seized on the opportunity to "get out of town," choosing the only acceptable alternative to living with her family and attending the junior college in her own community—a Nazarene college hundreds of miles from home.

PLAYING A ROLE

At Nazarene college, Adrian and her friends played the part of dutiful disciples of the church. "We went to chapel. We tithed. We taught Sunday school. We went to church. We did it and did it and did it to the bitter end...but for me, by then, it was a put on." Viewed through the lens of her years of self-study, compounded by whatever strands of free thinking she could glean from her studies, the church community, whether in Jerusalem, central California or her new university environment, came down to simply this: "Egos in conflict with each other." The real value of the college experience was to put a stamp on what Adrian calls "intellectual respectability so that there could be no question about my value as a human being." For Adrian, as for myself and Teresa, education—even if delivered within a fundamentalist environment—was the initiation of the long path leading to the reclamation of self-esteem: the central ingredient in the healing of Eve.

For Adrian, college was just the beginning of her negotiation of the layers that obscured her authentic self. "Even with my B.A. in education, I was still a female, Armenian immigrant, an outsider who didn't quite fit anywhere." Still searching, Adrian moved to Boston. "Someone turned me on to Trinity Episcopalian Church in Boston, a remarkable experience. The Rector, Theodore Parker Ferris, held liberal views...something that even the hint of in my father and mother's take on morality would have been a ticket straight to hell. I could see right through this—to see the light that Ferris was bringing to people. He was sharing his light and it was there for you to take, nobody twisting your arm to believe this or that." It was in the heart of the anti-Vietnam War era, and Adrian relished the fact that Ferris took firm moral stands on the issues, arriving at his views through the full utilization of his own moral conscience rather than through the authority of the Bible.

SPEAKING THE TRUTH IN HER HEART

"This was a monumental experience...worshipping side by side with Boston dowagers in their fur coats, homosexuals, college students and teenagers in blue jeans. Ferris set up an environment where we saw through the trappings and got a glimpse of each other's authentic selves. All different kinds of people—races, social classes, ages, religious backgrounds—accepted each other in this community." Adrian was so moved; she chose to be confirmed by Ferris. Unlike fundamentalist confession—with its impersonal language of shame and sin—Ferris's Episcopal confession asked only of Adrian that she speak the truth in her heart. "I loved that confession. It was really personal, not the collective, rote admission of sinfulness, but the sharing of one's inner light with the community."

While living in Boston, Adrian got a job teaching high school. Relying on her college references, the job she applied for and won was at a fundamentalist Christian school. Her two worlds—old and new—were colliding. A "Vote for Eldridge Cleaver" bumper sticker on the rear bumper of her Datsun attracted unwanted attention from her principal. Soon rumors began circulating in the school community that she drank wine on occasion—a big no-no—and that she was engaging in premarital sex. "That was the biggest laugh!" She smiled in the retelling, the first time during the course of our intense conversation. "The students were all screwing each other like rabbits and I was the virgin who was being accused of heinous sins." The "coup de grace" for Adrian was when she took her class of seniors to see Romeo and Juliet. It took a year—but ultimately she was fired.

"Painful as it was, the whole school episode was liberating. This was not only because it set me firmly on course away from my past, but also because through the eyes of the students, I could glimpse the future. They weren't that much younger than I and yet they didn't think twice about breaking the rules. The kids were playing Bob Dylan and protesting the war. I could see a major change in the kids coming up behind me and realized that if they could break the rules and survive, the earth wouldn't open up and swallow me either."

THE MOVE TO NEW YORK

A new job opportunity beckoned Adrian to move to New York. Because she was still emotionally attached to her Boston church, and still wary of male hierarchies that dominated most churches, she was in no hurry to find a replacement. Instead, she decided to take a break from organized religion. "My parents were kind of fuzzy about the Boston church and how and why I had been fired from my job, but they always assumed that I was going through some kind of phase and would come back and rejoin the family and church community. None of my sisters had left and it was just the expectation that I would return. When I moved to New York, it began to dawn on them—and me, as well—that there was no going back."

Another defining moment occurred soon after Adrian moved to New York. The phone rang. On the line was an old college friend who was stopping in New York on her way to Europe. Mary asked Adrian if she could stay at her apartment for a few nights. Adrian blanched, thinking of the apparent piety of her college days. This was a fellow dormitory resident with whom she had spent many hours in prayer. Now, looking around her Bohemian apartment, Adrian realized that she had broken just about every one of the fundamentalist prohibitions...even a few she hadn't yet committed when fired from her high school job.

"Compared to the girl she'd known in college, here I was in Sodom and Gomorrah itself. I smoked, I drank, I swore. But that wasn't the whole story. I had begun learning how to stand on my own two feet; I was writing my first book, voting my conscience, entertaining friends who would not have been acceptable before. I loved my unfolding relationships with all kinds of people, reading voraciously, enjoying the arts without judging them as wicked. Life had become my life—not somebody else's. So I thought to myself: Well, we'll just swing it...Mary gets the whole package or nothing at all."

Mary met Adrian at her office at the advertising agency in downtown Manhattan and the first thing Adrian did was take her to the Top of the Sixes for cocktails. Adrian assumed she would be shocked. Instead, Mary ordered a gin and tonic and they were off and running. As it turns out, Mary had gotten married right out of college—and divorced right after that, "the biggest no-no of all."

"Even though I will probably always feel myself to be an outsider, outside fundamentalism, outside organized religion, an immigrant outside the native-born population and an outsider even to my family of origin itself, I no longer felt alone." Bolstered by the encounter, Adrian confronted her parents with the truth. The conversation didn't go well.

"My mother was devastated by my leaving everything behind. It saddens me that it means so much to her. For her own peace of mind, she wants to know that when she and my father die, I'll be in heaven with them. It's not really about what's best for me, but what they want for themselves. I so want to say: 'Mom, there are so many bigger things to worry about. Do you want me to give you something real to worry about? Alright, but don't worry about this.'"

PRODUCTS OF OUR PAST

Adrian and I had spoken all afternoon and now the evening fog was rolling in. We continued our conversation over dinner in the elegant restaurant downstairs. Adrian ordered a glass of wine while I asked for iced tea. Having bonded over the lengthy conversation, we laughed easily together about my choice, because after all these years, I still have never been able to take one sip of alcohol. We both recognized that regardless of how far we'd come, we are still, sometimes in significant ways—sometimes in the silliest details—products of our environments. In fact, we had cause to laugh again just moments later when the first course of salads arrived. I took up my fork right away while Adrian paused to say an incongruous "bless this food" before digging in.

"So what is it that you worry about? What are you major concerns today?"

Adrian put her fork down, and then replied.

"In terms of being a product of my environment: I guess you'd have to say that I'm still extremely angry about the shame I was made to feel as a child and that I recently realized continues to be a problem for me." Adrian paused again, sizing me up. Then, taking a deep breath, decided that she could share her deepest concerns with me. As it turns out, because of some issues that had arisen in her workplace, Adrian had gone into therapy and was coming to grips with some behaviors that to her chagrin echoed some of the very issues she thought she had put long behind her. In brief, she had come to realize that in her management style, she had been making people feel ashamed of themselves as the means to enhancing productivity. Now, aware of how closely her management pattern mirrored her father's humiliating manipulations, she had become deeply ashamed of herself. Unwittingly, she had taken on the shame and guilt of the sinning Eve.

"I had this monumental amount of self-hate that I wasn't even aware of, bubbling beneath the surface. Therapy is extremely helpful because it's about getting to know all the things that you are: the building blocks that have contributed to both the good and destructive aspects of your personality. When you can see your patterns, you can make choices. I mean, you can make decisions along the way like if you are a messy housekeeper, that's not something you are going to be ashamed of: you are just going to be a messy housekeeper and carry on. You may be ashamed of not having your lipstick on right. That shame can lead you to excusing yourself to go to the lady's room and fixing it. I think growing up is deciding what you are going to be shamed by and what you are going to toughen up about. The real sin is taking it all on as if what Eve did has marked you, too."

DIFFERENT LAYERS

Over our main courses, Adrian shared some of her therapist's helpful perspective. "She taught me that we consist of different layers. Some of the layers are the products of our childhoods: like the original shame that has been built into the bedrock of my emotional makeup. But there wasn't only shame. There were good things, too. Even if it was painful for me as a child, I learned how important it is to set high ethical and moral standards. But then, at some point, you begin moving away from the bosom of your family and your own choices begin forming new layers. Like reputation. Reputations are built on what you do and who you are over time.

In my case, I had the reputation of being both an outstanding, reliable professional with impeccable standards—and someone who was hard to work for. People I didn't know knew me have an idea of what kind of person I am. What they didn't know is how and why my background and choices have formed me. In fact, until I entered into therapy, I wasn't clear about it, either. The more the building blocks and layers become visible to me, the easier it is for me to make choices that will be most beneficial to me, both professionally and personally."

Authenticity and integrity are the big pieces for Adrian now... the things, as she had suggested to her mother, "worth worrying about."

"To me, integrity means having the nerve and courage to do and be the right thing, even when it requires some kind of sacrifice or puts you into discomfort or even danger. This is something that is easier said than done, as both in my business and professional lives, it is so much more comfortable to look for a way out or around a difficult moral or ethical issue and not even notice that you've cut a corner."

"Do you ever miss black and white rules of religion?" I probed.

"Well, never the kind of stupid, mindless way important and unimportant things were mixed up together in the church I grew up in. But there is some kind of positive force in religion stirring beneath the surface. At least religion has thought about what it means to be and do good, even if it gets it wrong so often. Occasionally, like in the Boston church, it actually breaks through to the surface. It takes a lot to have organized religion work: to be a creative building thing rather than a destructive thing."

I asked Adrian if she had ever found another church to join. After all, she was one of the few co-researchers who had dipped back into organized religion—however briefly—and had a positive experience. Earlier in the day, I reminded her, she had explained that when she left Boston and moved to New York, it was the demands of her career and her emotional attachment to the church in Boston that had cooled her search.

Having conversed our way through so many layers, Adrian surprised me—as well as herself—with a sudden burst of self-revelation.

"I loved that church in Boston. But as I replay the community ethos, I realize that down deep, I was still an outsider. I mean, they were committed to living out of the spirit of Christ in its purest, most heart-felt expression. Jesus taught that you should do unto others as you would have them do unto you. That seems simple. But for me, there was a huge block. The problem with loving your neighbor as yourself is that it is based on the notion that you love yourself in the first place. Loving myself is something I am just now getting a handle on. After all, I grew up in a fundamentalist church that had a very different interpretation of the golden rule: 'Have no self-love and give it all away!' No wonder I've been less than motivated to rejoin a church."

RIGHTEOUS INDIGNATION

Over coffee, I inwardly recalled the apparently self-confident woman who had greeted me hours before. I remembered feeling intimidated by Adrian's firm handshake and blunt responses. Now, I appreciated the complexity of her life—admiring her ability to walk the talk of her authenticity. Through the veneer of her commanding presence, I now recognized a vulnerable quality about her that seemed more precious to me than high self-esteem. In fact, it was at this point during my interview with Adrian, that I recognized the importance of authenticity as a precursor to the reclamation of self-love.

As impressed as I was with Adrian's self-revelations, the best was yet to come. You may recall earlier, that psychologists have proposed that the antidote to anger is engagement in activities that lead to a sense of greater control over your environment. Adrian had done the hard work of reclaiming art, relationship, job and authenticity in her life. But the anger remained. For years, she had struggled with her anger—seeing it, at least, as some kind of advancement over the depression that had cast a pall over her childhood. But again, the anger persisted. Then, with the help of her therapist, she came to understand that like shame, anger was one of her core building blocks. She was going to have to learn to live with it—but not to let it call the shots. She could now be free to make choices in regard to what she should be angry about. Adrian had discovered one of her greatest pleasures—and what she was just beginning to recognize as the key to the unlocking of her true wisdom and power: righteous indignation.

"Watching the impeachment efforts directed toward Bill Clinton, I really got it in my gut: what fundamentalism had done to me was not personal. This is a huge problem on the national and now we realize, as unfortunate global events have unfolded, international level: "men of God" who have irrational control over their flocks who are a danger to both the individual and to society. These people—the Swaggerts, the Bakkers, the clerics, gurus and masters from all kinds of fundamentalisms—they are totally driven by corrupt emotions and a lust for manipulation. I deeply resent that they take what should be a spiritual experience and make it into a political, personal, abhorrent power play. I think they are evil. They are to be feared. Think of the Spanish Inquisition: we have leaders now who are rigidly entrenched in their own points of view. They are like a cult, doing whatever they can to cut their followers off from outside, alternative realities. I am grateful every day that despite these kinds of influences, I somehow have broken free to create a life of meaning. I have a moral, ethical point of view that is mine and I would never think of imposing my views on anyone else."

POLITICAL AWARENESS

Just as a heightened moral and ethical sensitivity can be traced to the rigidity of her upbringing in fundamentalism, so did Adrian's childhood bear another unexpected gift: political awareness. "There I was, a fundamentalist Christian in what we saw as our Jesus' city. But at the same time, Jerusalem was a Muslim city. Then there was the Catholic piece and the Orthodox piece and the Jewish piece, and they all seemed to be really serious about what they were doing. They were fighting over every inch of the land. I went to my religion's version of a school, but the question I was too young to formulate but that has colored my entire life was: "Who is really right here, and how does anybody know. Ultimately, what does it matter?"

Adrian had worked hard to reclaim the hidden layers of her life, revealing depositories of both pain and joyous authenticity. In Adrian's case—and for many of my co-researchers—that work includes not only negotiating the layers of shame and fear, but depression about the shame and fear, as well. And that's not all. As the psychologists point out, beneath depression repressed anger is hidden. Through therapy—and her own repressible spirit—Adrian had discovered that the healing process includes finding a healthy way both to experience and to express appropriate anger. That has been Adrian's challenge and journey. Blessedly, for Adrian, the anger is no longer turned inward. Rather, Adrian has given herself the gift of access to the secret source of her power: righteous anger fueled by her personal, societal, national and global concern for the impact of fundamentalism.

"For women raised in fundamentalism, the challenge is to differentiate how one sees one's self from how the world sees us. In the best of times and circumstances, the two merge. There is a synthesis, a wholeness that could be called the ultimate integrity. For women raised in fundamentalism, there is no way that we can go back to our original community—physically or emotionally—and find this ideal integrity. There will always be this sense of loss—the dream of a meaningful community that was wasted. We look to the present, making the choice to surround ourselves with friends who at least have the potential to see who we really are. We live in a time when our friends are more honest with us than they used to be in a caring way and will point out to you the places where you fall short. I am very lucky to have friends like this."

DO YOU BELIEVE IN GOD?

Long after our plates had been cleared, we were both reluctant to part. I thought of one last question, and it was a big one: Do you believe in God?

"Well, I don't use words like Higher Power or God, although I do talk to my plants, which says something about the issue. The thing is, since critical thinking doesn't help me, I can't say that there is a God, but I can't say there isn't, either. I do confess that seeing where I've come from and where my life has gone, I feel that somebody is taking care of me: that there is some sort of power and that I'm not alone. After years and years living in hell, something took over my life and I have a sense of confidence and restfulness—

the certainty that I just have to live my life day by day and that life will take care of itself. It's real and I have experienced it without my having to control it, manipulate it, run it. I let it go. We aren't really running our lives, you know?"

"Is there anything else?"

"Just this," Adrian replied. "It's not that I don't have self-doubts sometimes. But now, even when I'm feeling negatively about myself, I always view myself as better than the church ever saw me. That's really something, isn't it!"

Adrian had certainly come a long way towards healing Eve. Talking about her childhood, I recognized that Adrian as well as Teresa, among my many other participants, had accomplished something that their fathers had not been able to achieve: to look beyond their religion for their salvation. Whether they were too weak or too embedded, their fathers stayed in their circumstances. Earlier in the interview, Adrian and I had talked about the fact that we were sorry that our fathers died without ever really knowing us; however, for survival, all of the participants in my research had somehow found the courage to look forward rather than back for completion. We walked, ran, flew, took a bus, hid in libraries, changed schools or moved to another community to claim our wisdom and authenticity—we are each of us, in our own way, breaking the ties that bind and claiming spiritual freedom for ourselves, at last.

CONCLUSION
Full Circle

The tree is in full bloom for all to gaze
Knows that it all comes together in mysterious ways.
JIMMY LAURA SMULL

SCENE ONE

The ten-year-old girl walks along the dirt path, holding her grandmother's hand as they make their way together to the rim of the Grand Canyon. Overwhelmed with the awesome beauty of the expanse before her, the young girl turns to her grandmother and whispers: "This must be where God lives." The grandmother holds their clasped hands to her granddaughter's heart and replies "And here, too." They stand together in silence, smiling.

SCENE TWO

The pueblo elder rises at dawn to meditate upon the *Breath*. After donning jeans and her favorite hand-beaded jacket, she jumps into her Jeep and heads for the university. After her lecture on the anthropology of the southwest Indian tribes, her office is swamped. Blond co-eds in the trendiest outfits wait patiently in line with students of various races and religions, anxious to spend more time with their wise and self-assured professor.

SCENE THREE

The thirtyish mother of two young sons answers her cell phone. Her new husband is on the line, just to tell her he loves her. The two young sons look on with concern, as their mother completes the call and bursts out in tears. "What's wrong, momma?" the older son asks. "Nothing, sweetheart. Nothing at all. I'm just not used to being loved for no reason." The three join together in a hug before heading into the ice cream store for a treat.

You may recognize hints of the three women featured in these scenes from stories told earlier in this book. The grandmother in the first scene is myself, the same Jimmy Laura Smull who at the age of ten had been terrified by her literal baptism into the world of Christian fundamentalism, feeling alone, vulnerable and scared to death. The wise elder is Teresa, the same young Native American girl whose long years of shame and regret had begun the day the missionaries had taken her mother shopping, her traditional beaded dress traded for a corset and church-sanctioned attire. The third is Robin, who just a year prior had overheard her sons' grandmother telling them that if their mother divorced their abusive father, her first husband, she would burn in hell. But if you do see hints of who we once were, you would also surely recognize each of us to be at a different, happier stage in our lives—transformed.

The three of us, and the many more women who participated in my research study, have each in our own way done the difficult work of healing Eve. If you have done the exercises shared in these pages, you, too, have worked hard, dug deep and found courage you did not know you had in you. What's more, you've had to counter the toxic blows to your self-esteem you have suffered at the hands of fundamentalism without the benefit of having mastered critical thinking skills and having negotiated the stages of psychological development at age-appropriate times in your life.

In piecing ourselves together, all of the women in my research study have had to confront head-on the accusations of sinfulness stemming from Eve's original transgression in the Garden of Eden. But this was only the beginning. We've had to overcome the taboo against questioning the authority of the Bible, deal with the confusion of contradictions, move beyond black and white thinking and perfectionism and, above all, face our fear about going to hell for doing so.

Along the way, we discovered the resources with which to reclaim an inner and outer integrity: making peace with both the programmed and reactive aspects of ourselves to become whole. The reclamation of our authenticity may not have come all at once; in fact, maybe we suspect that we still have a ways to go. But at least we now know what it means to have the freedom to create a more meaningful life. Taken as a group, we have resolutely turned our backs on religious dogma. What we now embrace is not within "walls". We celebrate, instead, our personal style of expressing our spiritual selves. This, indeed, is the happy ending I promised you at the beginning of this process.

But now that we have achieved freedom for ourselves, we realize that there are others we have left behind. As I've traveled the country collecting and sharing my research, I have spoken heart to heart with women struggling to break free from fundamentalist versions of Catholicism, Islam and Judaism, religions that share the story of Adam and Eve. In addition, there are numerous non-Judeo-Christian communities—everything from psychological cults to UFO sects—which can be counted on to keep the issue of fundamentalism in the news on a daily basis.

While my formal research study centered on Protestant-based environments, you don't need to look any further than today's headlines to realize that every day, women trapped in various forms of fundamentalism around the globe are suffering physical, emotional and spiritual abuse. In America, the story of Elizabeth Smart opened a crack into the violence against women inherent in the extremities of Mormonism. News about the status of women coming out of the Middle East headline the list of global hot spots as terrorism concerns bring us face to face with the impact of Islamic fundamentalism on women and children.

Continuing the conversation concerning the harmful effects of extreme punitive discipline on our children begun in chapter eight, it is an understatement to say that the combination of idealistic youth raised in toxic fundamentalist environments of absolute truth bolstered by rigid rules of conduct has turned lethal. Many of these children have been routinely "hurt on purpose by an adult in order to teach a lesson in discipline, but the child experiences this pain and reproach as an assault upon the self as well as upon the body. Often the result is not only anger but also hatred and a powerful desire to revenge..." writes Dr. Eli Chesen. Chillingly, Chesen observes that whereas love in a child is natural, hatred is created. Dr. Missildine concurs that a child to whom the "rod" has been applied "may thus be forced to silence his protests and to obey and at that moment he learns to hate."

Every day, many in a new generation of sons and daughters around the world think not about living—but of killing and dying: be it the rebellious child of a fundamentalist Christian minister who decides to murder his classmates in a cloud of rage, or the teenaged student handed a gold key in religion class—told by fundamentalist clerics that if she is brave enough to become a suicide bomber, it will open wide the gates to heaven.

The research laid bare in this book gives us the information we need as a society to understand the inner working of all fanatic religious organizations and why it is that God-fearing children can grow up to become walking time bombs.

I conclude, then, with a call to action. We have shown that despite the odds stacked against us, we are not helpless. And the quest for the freedom we seek—not only for ourselves, but for us all—is not hopeless. We can begin in our own communities, reaching out to the women who have been left behind in living hells. We can help each other, and offer group opportunities to work through the exercises I've shared with you in this book. At the same time, we can reach out beyond our immediate environments to support the work of international women's rights groups, understanding better than anyone the link between systems that repress women, and the fate of their children who are raised learning to hate. By remembering to honor how hard we've worked to make it this far—and humbly admitting how far there is yet to go—we continue to help each other on our journeys to the establishment of a healthier life and world.

But it is not only women who have been affected by fundamentalism who are called to act. The churches and religious institutions to which we were entrusted bear the primary responsibility for our unnecessary pain, and it is to them that my final appeal is directed. To our religious leaders: note that all of the women in my study have left the church. These are brilliant, passionate, loving, caring women. This did not have to happen. You didn't have to lose any of the gifted women profiled in this book, nor any of the millions of others struggling to break free. So to the fundamentalist fathers and the toxic communities they have parented, I direct my final, most heartfelt plea. We are your daughters, your wives, your mothers. And in the name of God's love, we deserve to be healed, not punished. In this final appeal, I call upon the fundamentalist communities and institutions, themselves, to search their own souls and rectify the damage that has been and continues to be done to women every day in the name of God. We can and must work together to Heal Eve.

BIBLIOGRAPHY

American Psychiatric Association. (1994). <u>Diagnostic and statistical manual of mental disorders</u> (4th ed. Rev). Washington, DC.

Angelou, M. (1969). <u>I know why the caged bird sings</u>. NY: Random House.

Ashmore, S. (1979). <u>Fundamentals of archaeology</u>. Menlo Park, CA: The Benjamin/Cummings Publishing Company.

Babinski, E. (1995). <u>Leaving the fold: testimonies of former fundamentalists</u>. Amherst, NY: Prometheus Books.

Barnhart, C., & Barnhart, R. (Ed.). (1982). <u>The World Book Dictionary</u> (17th Ed.). NY: Doubleday & Company.

Berger, P. (1967). <u>The sacred canopy: elements of a sociological theory of religion</u>. NY: Doubleday & Company, Inc.

Bond, D. (1993). <u>Living myth: personal meaning as a way of life</u>. Boston, MA: Shambhala Publications.

Bradshaw, J. (1988). <u>Healing the shame that binds you</u>. Deerfield Beach, FL: Health Communications, Inc.

Bridges, W. (1980). <u>Transitions: making sense of life's changes</u>. Cambridge, MA: Perseus Books.

Campbell, D. (1977). <u>How to really love your child</u>. Wheaton, IL: Victor Books.

Chesen, E. (1972). <u>Religion may be hazardous to your health</u>. NY: Peter H. Wyden, Inc.

Criswell, W. (1980). <u>The doctrine of the church</u>. Nashville, TN: Convention Press.

De Beauvoir, S. (1952). <u>The second sex</u>. NY: Alfred A. Knopf.

Dyer, W. (2001). <u>10 Secrets for success and inner peace</u>. Carlsbad, CA: Hay House, Inc.

Eisler, R. (1987). <u>The chalice and the blade</u>. San Francisco, CA: Harper & Row.

Ellerbe, H. (1995). <u>The dark side of Christian history</u>. Orlando, FL: Morningstar and Lark.

Erikson, E. (1950). <u>Childhood and society</u>. NY: W. W. Norton & Company.

Erikson, E. (1968). <u>Identity: youth and crisis</u>. NY: W. W. Norton & Company.

Fawcet, J., & Nageli, H. (1940). Blest be the tie. In B. B. McKinney (Ed.), <u>The Broadman Hymnal</u> (p. 239). Nashville, TN: Broadman Press. (Original work published 1772.)

Feinstein, D., & Krippner, S. (1988). <u>Personal mythology: the psychology of your evolving self</u>. Los Angeles, CA: Jeremy P. Tarcher.

Feinstein, D., & Krippner, S. (1997). <u>The mythic path: discovering the guiding stories of your past—creating a vision for your future</u>. NY: Putnam/Jeremy P. Tarcher.

Friesema, W. (1995, fall). No room for doubt: former fundamentalists in psychotherapy. <u>Turning Wheel</u>, pp. 29–31.

Greven, P. (1977). <u>The protestant temperament: patterns of child-rearing, religious experience, and the self in early America</u>. NY: Alfred A. Knopf.

Greven, P. (1991). <u>Spare the child: the roots of punishment and the psychological impact of physical abuse</u>. NY: Alfred A. Knopf.

Havighurst, R., & Keating, B. (1990). The religion of youth. In M. Strommen (Ed.), <u>Research on religious development: a comprehensive handbook</u>. NY: Hawthorn Books.

Hesse, H. (1951). <u>Siddhartha</u>. NY: New Directions.

Hicks, J., & Hicks, E. (2001). <u>A new beginning II: a personal handbook to enhance your life, liberty and pursuit of happiness</u>. San Antonio, TX: Abraham-Hicks Publications.

Holy Bible: King James Version. (1972). Camden, NJ: Thomas Nelson.

Holy Bible: Authorized King James Version. (1976). Wheaton, IL: Tyndale House Publishers.

Hudson, R., & Watts, I. (1996). At the cross. The Best Gospel Songs Ever. Milwaukee, WI: Hal Leonard Corporation. (Original work published in 1885.)

Kleefeld, C. (1998). The alchemy of possibility: reinventing your personal mythology. Carmel, CA: Merrill-West Publishing Co.

Krakauer, J. (2003). Under the banner of heaven: a story of violent faith. NY: Doubleday.

Larsen, S. (1996). The mythic imagination: the quest for meaning through personal mythology. Rochester, VT: Inner Traditions International.

Lowe, J. (1998). Oprah Winfrey speaks. NY: John Wiley & Sons, Inc.

Maltz, M. (1960). Psycho-cybernetics. Englewood Cliffs, NJ: Pocket Books.

Maslow, A. (1964). Religions, values and peak experiences. NY: Penguin.

Meehl, J. (1995). The recovering Catholic: personal journeys of women who left the church. Amherst, NY: Prometheus Books.

Miller, A. (1983). For your own good: hidden cruelty in child-rearing and the roots of violence. (Hildegarde and Hunter Hannum, Trans.). NY: Farrar, Straus, Giroux.

Missildine, W. H. (1963). Your inner child of the past. NY: Simon & Schuster.

Niebuhr, G. (1998, June 10). Southern Baptists declare wife should "submit" to her husband: denomination moves to emphasize family life. The New York Times, pp. 1, 20.

Northrup, C. (1998). <u>Women's bodies, women's wisdom: creating physical and emotional health and healing</u>. NY: Bantam Books.

Nunn, C. (1964). Child-control through "coalition with God." <u>Child Development</u>, 35, pp. 429–432.

Peale, N. (1956). <u>The power of positive thinking</u>. NY: Ballantine Books.

Piaget, J. (1952). <u>The origins of intelligence in children</u>. NY: International Universities Press, Inc.

Piaget, J. (1954). <u>The construction of reality in the child</u>. (M. Cook, Trans.). NY: Basic Books.

Piaget, J. (1977). <u>The moral judgment of the child</u>. NY: Penguin Books.

Rand, A. (1943). <u>The fountainhead</u>. NY: Macmillan Publishing Company.

Rand, A. (1957). <u>Atlas shrugged</u>. NY: Random House.

Ritter, K., & O'Neill, C. (1996). <u>Righteous religion: unmasking the illusions of fundamentalism and authoritarian Catholicism</u>. NY: Haworth Pastoral Press.

Ruether, R. (1983). <u>Sexism and God-talk: toward a feminist theology</u>. Boston, MA: Beacon Press.

Seligman, M.E.P. (1992). Learned helplessness. In T. Costello and J. Costello, <u>Abnormal Psychology</u> (2nd Ed.). NY: HarperCollins.

Shinn, F. (1925). <u>The game of life and how to play it</u>. Marina del Rey, CA: De Vorss & Company.

Smull, J. (1996). <u>The experience of disillusionment with one's personal mythology: a heuristic study</u>. Unpublished manuscript. San Francisco, CA: Saybrook Institute.

Spock, B., & Rothenberg, M. (1985). <u>Baby and child care</u>. NY: Pocket Books.

Spong, J. (1991). <u>Rescuing the Bible from fundamentalism: a bishop rethinks the meaning of scripture</u>. San Francisco, CA: HarperCollins.

Stone, M. (1976). <u>When God was a woman</u>. NY: Harcourt Brace Jovanovich.

Smith, M. (1975). <u>When I say no I feel guilty</u>. NY: Bantam Books.

Tavris, Carol. (1992). <u>The mismeasure of woman</u>. NY: Simon and Schuster.

<u>The American Heritage College Dictionary</u> (1993).(3rd Ed.). NY: Houghton Mifflin Co.

Winell, Marlene. (1994). <u>Leaving the fold</u>. NY: New Harbinger.

Wulff, D. (1991). <u>Psychology of religion</u>. NY: Wiley.